# Creating the
# National Environmental
# Master Plan–2006

Also by John Tettemer

*Who Speaks for the Trees?*

*The Six Principles of Creative Problem-Solving*

# Creating the National Environmental Master Plan–2006

## Including the Ten Required Action Steps

### John M. Tettemer, P.E.

JUNIPER SPRINGS PRESS

JUNIPER SPRINGS PRESS
P.O. Box 1385, Apple Valley, CA 92307
Internet: www.JuniperSpringsPress.com
For information, e-mail: Publish@JuniperSpringsPress.com

© 2005 by The Tettemer Family Trust dated November 6, 2001

ISBN-13: 978-0-9678876-6-1
ISBN-10: 0-9678876-6-6
Library of Congress Control Number: 2005930148

All rights reserved. No part of this book may be reproduced in any form or by any electronic or mechanical means, including information storage and retrieval systems, without permission in writing from the publisher, except by a reviewer, who may quote brief passages in a review.

Printed and bound in the United States of America

First printing: August 2005

# Contents

| | |
|---|---|
| **Introduction** | vii |
| Personal Thoughts | ix |
| **I  A CHECKERED PAST** | |
| Our Evolving Relationship with Nature | 1 |
| Action Was Required | 6 |
| What Naturally Evolved: Gravel in the Gears | 13 |
| **II  WHERE ARE WE?** | |
| We Have Lost Our Way | 21 |
| Attitude Changes: Who Speaks for the Trees? | 26 |
| **III  A BETTER CHOICE** | |
| Saying It . . . My New Orleans Manifesto | 29 |
| Stepping Back to See How Nature Works | 48 |
| Surprising Soul-Mates | 52 |
| Contrasting Possibilities: Primal Choices | 53 |
| **IV  THE HIGH ROAD** | |
| Grounding the Vision—Having Chosen the High Road | 59 |
| Preparing Ourselves for Success . . . **The Ten Action Steps** | 65 |
| Rising High Enough to See: The Las Vegas Inspiration | 67 |
| Adopting the Model | 89 |
| Master Planning an Entire Community | 92 |

V  GETTING SPECIFIC
    Recruiting a Leader                                    95
    Applying the Model . . . Preparing for Action           97

A Final Word or Two                                       105
Epilog                                                    111

About the Author                                          113

# Introduction

In one way or another, we all recognize that we rely on Nature for our very survival. We also recognize the value of having clean air and clean water . . . clean rivers and oceans . . . and natural wildlife areas. In the rush of daily life, though, we may easily lose our connection with those basic aspects of Nature. But that seems okay, since we know we've assigned the job of caring for natural values and of understanding environmental issues to various responsible others . . . mainly government and various advocacy groups.

In many respects, having government agencies look after the environment has been a step in the right direction. As we shall see, though, it has led us to where we find ourselves today . . . with many people concerned that the system we've relied upon until now has become outdated.

In the past, for very logical reasons, we adopted the quick-fix approach of government *regulation*. It sounded good, and for a while it was, because it controlled or even stopped damaging or potentially damaging activities. Unfortunately, however, those same regulations have become top-heavy and burdensome, leaving almost no room for innovation and flexibility. They don't allow for change that might improve our relationship to the environment over the long haul. They don't allow us to pursue excellence.

But there is a viable alternative, and that's what this book is about. That alternative is a *Master Plan* approach, a method of environmental management that encourages flexible, innovative, sensitive, regional planning that treats ourselves and Nature as partners, and uses that partnership in creative, responsive, forward-thinking ways.

Is that an impossible goal? Absolutely not, because *today*, in spite of the existing regulatory system, there are many excellent regional environmental plans that provide examples of how we can proceed. Further, they can be adopted as segments of a national Master Plan that reflects our best expectations of the future, not based on regulation but on a cooperative, collaborative vision of a sustainable relationship between ourselves and Nature, everywhere in these United States. That Master Plan is what we will be looking at in the following pages.

# Personal Thoughts

As I sit down to write this book, I am well aware of my personal feelings about the environment, which to me is best defined simply as "the place where we humans live." We are obviously totally dependent on our environment, the physical-biological world around us, for our very existence ... the soil ... the air ... water ... trees ... plants ... and countless natural processes, most of which we don't really understand, yet for our safety and satisfaction we try to control.

Nature—this environment that surrounds us—deserves our full attention and respect! The recent tsunami in Southeast Asia is a reminder about the power of Nature and the importance of respecting natural forces at all levels.

Does giving attention and respect to Nature mean we should all return to the land, rub sticks together to make fire, become vegetarians, do Yoga, or carry no-growth banners? Not at all! It *does* involve applying huge doses of common sense to our relationship with Nature, so what we do will serve our endeavors and Nature's needs.

There are some things we can do to take the first simple steps toward reconnecting with Nature ... to honestly *define* a mutually respectful relationship ... one where the health and interrelationship of both is acknowledged and is a basic given. Not to prohibit development, not to turn our lands into nature preserves ... but to take informed baby-steps ... a commonsense move toward planning the future for natural processes and for man's activities that respects both . . . a *Master Plan* that simply says "this is for you" and "this is for us" . . . a clear line that both sides can rely on.

It means moving the environment back onto center stage, planning our relationship with it by opening our eyes and redefining this relationship in a way that's based on proven successes in the "real world," while fully respecting Nature's needs. That is what I have to offer . . . shedding a light on how the path we have all been on for centuries has recently been subtly altered and how we are now called to the noble and challenging task of reshaping our world and ourselves to match this new reality—an exciting opportunity for all of us.

Thinking bigger and exchanging the conflicts within the existing system for a collaborative effort in support of a Master Plan is timely. My purpose in this small book is to relate some stories that help set the stage for that. From my personal experiences, I will examine the institutional sticking points that currently prevent improving our stewardship of our environment. Then I will prescribe simple and timely steps that can be taken to change our current system to one that embraces our ideals and redirects our fascination with conflict to an approach based on collaboration . . . that steers available resources away from distrust and toward support of our true partner, Nature . . . Mother Earth. This will require a Master Planning effort to create a map, a Guidance Document, that sets forth—in detail—objectives for our land and water . . . a National Environmental Master Plan.

I will also describe the aspects of my personal and professional background that made me into an environmentalist—or rather, that led to the rebirth of the environmentalist who was already within me. In an engineering career that was devoted largely to innovation and the application of new ideas to large-scale flood control, water conservation, and wetlands systems, I became intensely aware of the environmental challenges of our time. Many of these challenges are homemade, related directly to the way we have chosen to assign environmental stewardship within government.

Taking note of these challenges motivated me to consider my own ways of seeing the big picture as I found solutions to large-scale regional water and environmental issues, and to notice that they could equally well be applied to much larger areas, specifically the entire country, in a national plan. That, in turn, has led me to boldly set forth a new path for our nation to follow: *a clear, specific, action-based prescription for developing what I call the National Environmental Master Plan–2006.*

My adult life has been spent in the practical world of engineering activities that, with vision, I have applied to the natural world of water and environmentally sensitive wetlands through complex, large-scale projects that pushed the state of the art. So I qualify as an "applied environmentalist," having worked both sides of the street . . . having worked with the interests of man and of Nature.[*]

In my most thoughtful times, when I consider the interrelationship of man and Nature, I sense that we have outgrown old relationships that served us both. We have lost touch in important ways. Nature needs our attention, and so we need to reexamine our relationship with her, so we can understand the great crisis of our times and, if we are selflessly wise, do something about it.

You may agree that much of what follows is like the story of the Wizard of Oz. You will recall that the various characters in that story were seeking to solve personal problems by going to the Wizard. We get to know each character well as the story unfolds; we sympathize with their circumstances and feel, as they do, that the answers to all their problems ultimately do lie with the Wizard.

And they have a clear map of the yellow brick road, which they follow wherever it leads. They find their way along it until they

---

[*] Readers wishing to learn more about my personal and professional background (as well as the unusual events surrounding the sudden, unexpected spiritual breakthroughs I experienced in midlife) may be interested in my full-length autobiography, *Who Speaks for the Trees?*, published in 2005 by Juniper Springs Press. Major portions of this book have been adapted from that work.

reach the Wizard ... and then, alas, they learn that the deep-throated, all-powerful, all-wise Wizard, once revealed by the dog, turns out to be just one of them, with all the same problems ... then they, and we, are sent home to do our work.

I like that story because it teaches us to not rely on a godlike personage or assembly of personages—government—to represent the interests of people or Nature without strong, clear guidance from those it is there to serve. Indeed, the crisis of our time comes about as we see that, through its natural evolution, government becomes a self-centered enterprise with antiquated ideas and stiff joints. Society collaborates through passive acceptance of the Oz-like nature of government ... all-powerful and all-knowing ... yet it is not in sync with the people's need for a plan that creates long-term assurances about land-use, a plan that meets all of man's expanding needs and also meets Nature's requirements.

This crisis demands change!

So I will pull back the curtain and suggest the need for some adjustments to our current circumstances, offering a new model that will change government's key underlying assumptions about managing our long-term relationship with Nature.

# I

# A CHECKERED PAST

*Our Evolving Relationship with Nature*

### *A Brief Review*

Some four hundred years ago, the first settlers from Europe arrived in this country. We can envision them encountering an extensive natural coastline, behind which virgin forests seem to stretch endlessly into the distance. The forests and clearings, with their occasional rivers and creeks, are a nearly ideal habitat where the wild, free processes of Nature can unfold.

Maybe my picture of things is idealized, but you get the point.

Then those settlers stepped ashore and began to re-create civilization. Trees were cleared to make room for what their wood might be used for: dwellings and other buildings, wagons, boats, tools, and of course firewood. Fields were planted, producing ample food if the weather cooperated. Animals, both wild and domesticated, were plentiful as sources of food, fur, and countless products for home and farm.

This, in my mind's eye, is a picture of the first Colonies—perhaps simplified, even idealized, but an overall view of basic conditions there.

Man learned to use what Nature had to offer, and it was abundant, readily available. So abundant, in fact, and so readily available that if the soil failed to produce like last year, an entirely new area could be selected for the next crop. There was land aplenty, with man and Nature closely attuned to each other. Survival required it. Nature was large and man was small, and the requirements of their attunement were well understood by man . . . and respected. All was fundamentally well.

As time went by, populations grew and spread. They had increased demands for Nature to fill, but she was ample in her bounty, giving forth plentifully.

Before long, word got back to the tradition-bound countries of Europe from which these settlers had come and even more people set forth to the Promised Land. Some came to the same coastal areas where those original settlers landed, while others went farther away and found rivers they could journey along before putting down roots—literal and metaphorical. They too found Nature abundant and ample, overflowing with bounty.

Humanity also moved to the interior, as the coasts, major rivers, and inland waterways were developed . . . land was cleared, fields planted, foot paths then cart paths and then roads developed, communities evolved, governments were installed.

Still, Nature was more than adequate, providing abundantly and even producing surpluses that could be stored or traded with others for goods or services. Some of these surpluses were even exported, as the new nation spilled and sailed across its borders. To provide the necessary ease of access, areas near waterways—coasts, rivers, and lakes—developed first, and most densely.

The demands on Nature continued to grow and grow and grow. Small communities became small cities, some with names we still know today. Small businesses became little industries. The combination of the people's energies, political and social freedom, and Nature's abundance was a powerful stimulant for growth. And growth followed—as surely as morning after night. More land was cleared for timber and agriculture, more fishing was done, more animals were killed for food and by-products, and also to protect livestock and other farm and ranch animals. Roads were built, followed by railroads and then industries using underground resources . . . coal and iron and more.

People made choices about their lives based on their communities' specialties, their family's skills, and the availability of new jobs, as specialization brought some off the farms into the cities. The smithy might go into town to work the steel factory, and would rely on buying food from his neighbor, as there was not time to grow his own.

You can see the map of the United States in your mind's eye. See the population spreading out, farming larger and larger areas. Notice the smokestacks and trains and caravans moving around . . . thus opening many new areas for habitation and related agriculture. There were also growing areas of specialization. Farmers farmed, harriers ran horse-drawn carts, miners mined, and so on. Urban populations started to grow. Family farming continued and served both rural and urban areas. Cattle, sheep, and other animals were raised for their meat and coats. There were more choices and the immigrants provided labor for city jobs.

Look again at a map of the United States in your mind's eye and see the coasts—west, east and gulf—attracting populations. See the river valleys, themselves transportation corridors, becoming populated. See the rangeland being used for livestock. See the railroads connecting the coasts. We are a long way now from the Colonies where we started.

During all of this growth and human business, Nature has been used, and she cooperated. There was a close relationship with and a respect for Nature in most cases. We relied on Nature and were well-aware of her contribution to our lives. It was, in general, a partnership. People knew where their food came from . . . maybe down the road at Bill's. Or the cattle we saw being driven down the street on the way to market—they would probably be in the butcher shop in a few days. We were closely connected . . . even in our growing towns.

These successes led to our having more people and more needs for Nature to satisfy—and our supply lines lengthened. Soon generations of youngsters grew up in cities and had little idea of what farming was like, what animal husbandry meant in practice. They were logically attending to the needs of their urbanizing lives, served through a growing network of stores. Little had changed in the rural and farm areas, yet much was about to change in the cities.

For as cities grew, local government changed from gatherings of farmers to meetings of local city folk, many of whom had not served with Nature on a farm or in a ranching community.

That was all as it should be, natural and logical.

As the cities grew and industrialization occurred, people began to gain sufficient wealth to have greater latitude about where communities were built. Why not live near the river? It's cool there during the summer, and we can fish and swim. The views are excellent. And again— logically—the prime locations became the preferred locations. Often these were areas where there was water nearby: rivers, lakes, oceans, or other lush, scenic properties. Note again in your mind that as these highly valued areas were developed, some of the natural values, including habitat values, were reduced or destroyed.

"There is plenty of Nature around for natural values and, anyway, this area is very special to me. I want to live here." This attitude became more and more prevalent, particularly among those who were disconnected from Nature and who failed to recognize that she was the fundamental provider in their lives.

Jumping forward in time until just after the Second World War, we see exponential growth in many areas of the United States. No one gave much thought to the *impact* of that growth, as though growth were a reward celebrating the end of the war. Lots of children, and lots of houses, and lots of new communities sprang forth. Things were on the edge of dramatic change. Urban demographics ruled the day at all levels of government. It was a huge party. And it had some interesting lessons to teach us about planning. We are still licking our wounds.

In the years that followed, two events were forcefully set in motion that would later come into my professional life.

*First*, was the recognition that locations ideal for urban growth were having a profound effect on locations of high environmental value. This was, in a way, a new idea: that man could not just continue to use the environment without showing care for its long-term future. Examples were all around us, from the destruction of nesting areas for migratory fowl to the filling of a slough deemed a mosquito nuisance without considering its value as a nursery for young fish that later went to sea and became food for growing communities. Larger habitat areas for animals that had adapted to a unique topography, or soil, or pond were soon paved over with homes and streets. Many creeks were placed underground in pipes, vanishing from the surface.

Many natural wetlands, often felt to be the womb of much natural life, vanished as well.

*Second*, there was a growing interest in developing property on all coasts and most waterways. It became evident that local officials were seeking and receiving handouts from the always-helpful Federal government to flood-proof areas that were subject to seasonal water damage. The dollar demands for help were growing faster each year, in spite of major public works projects intended to solve flooding problems and thereby eliminate the demands.

Something was clearly wrong.

We seek to understand why. Maybe we have become too disconnected from our roots in Nature . . . in natural processes. Perhaps we have moved to simple linear cause-and-effect thinking that leaves little room for the dominant acts of Nature, which means we don't fully understand what's going on. Our best thinking seems based on personal, societal, and cultural self-interest in support of materialism. Materialism is excellent and it serves us . . . until it changes from a system that supports what we do to a system that, as though it were a religion, dominates, determines, and governs what we do . . . a basis for separating ourselves from others . . . starting to harden our hearts in the name of competition for scarce resources.

It may be only a matter of time before Nature rebels to remind us—with the awesome power only she can muster—that we humans are not solely in charge of determining the future of this small speck of dust we call planet Earth . . . .

And so, we are getting to the place where we take Nature and our Earth for granted to the extent that a naïve onlooker might believe we have artificial ways to produce anything we want, or—in a pinch—to buy it from others who get it from "somewhere" . . . all of this with total disregard for the simple fact that we are completely dependent on the natural and harmonious functioning of this Earth. We need Nature—not once a month or once a week but . . . every day! Many of us act as though we have become more important than Nature and her environment. *We act as though we are bigger and she is smaller.* That is a dangerous assumption, a perilous way of living to adopt. It is incorrect and can have serious repercussions.

As we shall see, these issues spawned two national initiatives . . . both of which are central to the message of this book.

## *Action Was Required*

In regard to the first issue—dealing with the effect of urban growth on locations of high environmental value—life became uneasy for those who were building new communities. Concerns began to be expressed about the location and impact of various housing and business developments. These concerns were raised by people who moved in last year and didn't want the values in their communities changed this year, as new subdivisions went in next door. Soon, resistance to additional "uncontrolled growth" developed and attracted the attention of the greater community. Much was heard about "urban sprawl." Scientists, academics, and advocacy groups became interested and started to speak out.

A new form of activism started locally in a few spots, and people who were interested in having "progress" stopped or slowed began paying attention to changes that were occurring in natural values. Though activists brought pressure to stop additional growth using environmental impact theories, local planning and building officials also felt landowner pressure and were unable to muster enough political and even legal support to stop the offending development. The tractors rumbled on ... the homes were bought ... and, as happens in many cycles, the very people who benefited most from having new homes and shopping centers became the voices for change to control development. In seeking such change, they found out that laws needed to be enacted if land development were to be curtailed in the "public interest." This struck deeply, down to matters that were fundamental to our nation's history, growth, and future: matters of private property rights vs. presumed public interest.

Local interests, however, were unable to stop what they deemed abusive use of important land. The influence of powerful local landowners was more than the local politicians could deal with ... and so in most cases they didn't.

Pressure mounted from many parts of the United States for action by the government to protect rivers, wetlands, and a number of animal species and habitats that were threatened or were even near extinction. Some local and state governments considered legislation and related enforcement actions that would be necessary to prevent further losses. Studies were made to define the locations and values of certain natural resources that required protection. But protection efforts were spotty and occurred mostly in response to specific, strident, local environmental interests.

Over time, local politicians passed the problem to the state governments by looking for solutions that involved the state. That was politically expedient. Each state then did what it thought best, and also the Federal government entered the picture. The politics around the environment moved to state houses and to Washington, where advocates could get more attention.

Many local advocates loved that and for a number of different reasons ... one being that they had greater influence over a large body like Congress, with its varied constituency and its long distance away from local communities. It was Oz-like, and yet there was no yellow brick road here.

The issues that polarized people most strongly involved environmental values related to water. That is where the highest values often are, and water-related values are simplest to show visually. A filled-in marsh is easy to see and vote against, even if its science is not understood.

As time passed, many state governments and the Federal government got active, drafting legislation to set in place systems to prevent negative effects on habitats deemed to be of value. Please note my saying that their intent was to *prevent* new damage to certain high-value habitats.

Legislation was adopted to create various national wetland and endangered species protection programs. Now a method to implement the legislation was required, and the Federal government assigned enforcement of new environmental regulations to a number of Federal agencies. The agencies accepted the new assignments, however they each saw those assignments in the context of their own specialties ... which led to conflicts ... for there was no *unifying* agency or legislation. A regulatory maze was created, with its attendant supporters, consultants, and political agendas.

There were no environmental police in the state and Federal governments, but soon they were found. Existing employees working on biological issues and dealing with habitat preservation and enhancement had new responsibilities added to their assignments and they became de facto policemen. I know many of them, and they were very unhappy. Agencies (such as the Federal Corps of Engineers) that dealt with waterways set up sections within their many districts. The U.S. Fish and Wildlife Service was brought in, as were many other Federal agencies, such as Marine Fisheries.

Various other agencies at the Federal level also became involved, since the laws indirectly affected their missions, and the table was set for confrontations among the agencies. In many areas, the same happened at the state level. Fish and Game Departments, Water Quality organizations, and numerous other state subdivisions got involved to protect their turf and attempt to fulfill their missions while also coping with power gained by still other state entities under the new rules. (There was and is competition within and between state and Federal agencies as well.)

These conflicts are not necessarily due to lack of competence of the staffs. They *are* due to the complete lack of clear objectives in dealing with the vast unknowns of Nature's processes and the resulting inability to adjust man's institutions to respond. The legislative guidance of "stop loss"—that is, attempting to prevent any negative impact on existing wetlands, high-value habitats, and species—is not an effective long-term planning strategy . . . though it is an attractive stopgap and easily voted for. The lack of objectives not only involves such things as water-quality standards for the fry of a particular fish species, but also the amount of habitat to be protected to assure the success of a target species. Very complex!

I have spent hours in discussions with extremely caring government biologists representing different agencies that tried to create a scientific record for how they were going to decide about the use of sensitive land worth many millions of dollars. The results were often negotiated and therefore lacked a scientific consensus. This sometimes caused applicant landowners great concern.

On this first issue, that of dealing with the effect of urban growth on locations of high environmental value, my years of experience strongly suggest that the regulatory processes that were started to deal with it and are now still in use—the national wetland and endangered species protection programs—were well-intended and appropriate, because they could be installed quickly and would presumably get the desired results. This is no longer the case, however.

On the second issue, that of building in areas subject to flood losses, Federal studies indicated that more money was being spent each year from the Federal budget to bail out local flood-prone communities, in spite of the funds that had already been spent for flood-control structures that presumably would prevent new flood losses. This made no sense and was clearly poor public policy. But why was it happening? The answer was simple. The locals happily took Federal funds for flood-control improvements and built projects, yet continued to allow development in high-flood hazard areas.

Something needed to be done! So a new program was initiated. It was the Federal Flood Insurance Program, which declares that each local community is to be mapped and flood-hazard areas in its jurisdiction identified, using Federal guidelines. Then development is to be restricted in those areas according to certain rules. It was essentially a template for national planning—a model for the nation to use—and it attracted local support, since it assured Federally subsidized flood insurance for a period of time. This program is important because it is a real-life model, which I will discuss later as part of addressing the existing lack of environmental planning in the United States.

The programs that were implemented to deal with these two issues have been extremely important and were entirely appropriate responses to the needs of the environment and to matters related to Federal involvement in local land-use management, as seen in the Flood Insurance Program. *Individuals in the general public have little or no understanding of either program, and if asked would indicate that they presume the right thing is being done through the regulatory programs to protect the environment and to minimize flood losses.*

### *Unusual Side Effects . . . The Exceptions*
The greater regulatory interest by the Federal and state governments in protecting environmentally important values had a won-

derful side-effect. Many communities as well as landowners, often of large tracts of land, could not see that their interests were being protected by the regulatory programs. They were accustomed to working with large acreages and were familiar with the idea that the land could be wisely dedicated to many uses. Almost all of these owners knew their land contained valuable natural assets, some of which might be subject to regulation. These lands often had important bodies of water or unusual vistas, represented complete ecosystems that needed very special planning, had some legally defined endangered species that were unique to their property or the region, or had historical significance of importance to the community. All of these special attributes needed to be addressed in a way that satisfied the local community, the local and state regulators, and the Federal agencies. As many as a dozen agencies might have had a legal interest in the use of an owner's land, and all exercised their unique and often competing interests through regulation. The owners, however, wanted long-term assurances and preservation of complex groupings of natural values, some of which were not regulated—in short, a regional plan.

Seeing that the regulatory system was not working the way they wanted it to be working, local landowners, advocates, and governments set out to do what the regulatory system doesn't . . . to envision a regional plan that protects or enhances environmental values and also defines man's compatible uses . . . a true regional vision.

Some exceptional plans were birthed from inspired local interests.

The regulations said, in effect, that each agency has the legal obligation to enforce certain laws related to its area of specialization, the rules of which might be in conflict with other agencies. If that were so, resolution could be based on the interaction of local personalities, who might try to work things out. The landowner or community was obliged to provide the agency or agencies with required technical information about proposed activities that were to be reviewed by the agency, to see if there was any environmental impact subject to its jurisdiction and if actions to protect against loss were adequate. If the agency was satisfied, the staff would issue a permit or other appropriate document. It was up to the landowner or the community to obtain all the other approvals that might be needed and respond to interagency problems.

For many small landowners, this form of regulation was overwhelming and very expensive, even if the potential environmental impacts were minimal. Within the "no-loss" policies, there was little room for alternatives, even if the environment would benefit. Many were discouraged by the limitation of the policies.

### *A Bright Light . . .*

In a relatively short time, it became evident that the regulatory process, though maybe okay as an initial Band-Aid, was not equipped to deal rationally with larger pieces of land, whole communities, or land with very complicated issues, because it was about piece-by-piece regulation . . . that is, the prevention of negative impacts, one-by-one, in specific geographical areas. It could not look beyond the area of direct impact to see the greater opportunities within the region. As an example, a very small wetland adjacent to a busy urban intersection may have limited long-term environmental benefit and yet must be preserved. A better solution would be to use the owner's funds to create an equivalent wetland on another property set aside for that long-term purpose. (We will talk more about this in a few pages.)

These regulations stimulated a new, unexpected response. A few highly motivated landowners or communities saw the regulations as *too limiting* and even inappropriate to their circumstance— that is, ineffective for managing the property involved. They set out to take their vision and create a master plan for the use of the land of interest. The plan included protection and often the enhancement of the environmental values of that land. The results were staggering. Many of the plans show great care for the environment and many are using the natural values to increase the attractiveness of the property. *All have the one attribute that they are based on stepping back to see the property as a whole, to see all of its attributes,* and creating a plan that recognizes the highest and best use of the land, including environmental protection.

What emerged were local, large-scale planning efforts that were so grand as to attract attention for their excellence. In the land, local advocates had seen wondrous ways to bring forward its natural values and still allow other uses by man. In many cases, these local plans generated a lot of local political attention that was noticed by the regulatory agencies. Local political pressures led in turn to pressure for exceptions to regulations where the general evidence was strong about the net environmental impacts of the overall planned area. These were high-risk endeavors for local interests, since there was no assurance that the rules could be tweaked until maybe years into the process. Some of the locally developed planning efforts became community causes, so strong in certain communities that new local agencies were established to administer them or new laws were passed to support their adoption, thereby complementing the regulatory legislation. Well-planned regional plans evolved and are beacons for all of us.

Many of these plans have developed around the United States. They stand as monuments to the courage and perseverance of motivated locals to apply common sense and overcome flaws in regulatory programs that had become evident when they discouraged community or regional planning.

A local model emerged . . . one of local excellence, from which we can learn a lot. We can use many, many more!

## *What Naturally Evolved: Gravel in the Gears*

Nearly all young endeavors start out with a burst of enthusiasm . . . of idealism . . . energized by their newness and their perception of the worthiness of their overall intention. If they are private endeavors, they can either bloom for a short period and succeed . . . or wither and die—depending on their ability to serve the purpose they were founded for or to evolve into something else. If they are government endeavors, however, the situation is quite different, since our society in no way expects a "succeed or die" approach from government (because the government, if it fails at something, is not obliged to quit doing it). What society does expect from government is—as necessary—rescue, salvation, the healing of wounds, repair jobs, or quick fixes . . . usually leading to the adoption of legislation that the public can rally around and that will receive the votes needed for approval.

Those quick fixes are born in committees and from that womb, where consensus rather than bold leadership tends to carry the day, they become, let us say, *average* in quality . . . seldom more. The members of those committees who have particular and pertinent concerns are heard, yet often they can't offer workable proposals that are any more effective than what has already been proposed legislatively and brought to them for consideration. And what is the legislative view of what the committee is reviewing? It is usually that the proposed legislation is feasible, addresses the problem, and is the best anyone can do. And if it needs to be modified later, it can be. Later.

And so it was for the earliest legislation aimed at protecting the "waters of the United States" and endangered species. It was a quick fix. It sought to stop abuse, period. It wasn't attempting to *create* anything at all. It was trying—through policing and through regulating—to solve a problem.

We now have ample evidence to indicate that we have outgrown this policing-and-regulatory approach, and for several reasons. To examine this evidence, we can revisit the legislation at Federal and state levels that seeks to protect the waters of the United States and endangered species. We can look at the gravel in the gears of the policing-and-regulatory machinery that's supposed to be protecting or enhancing the environment through regulatory processes. (I must point out that what I am proposing is not *deregulation*. Rather, it is a specific *alternative* form of regulation.)

In summary, I am motivated to suggest change because:

- The laws are fundamentally designed to try to police potential abuses. This sets up an adversarial policy.
- The laws focus only on land defined as "water" or habitat for special species we currently know about.
- The process is fear-based and, as such, does not lend itself to creative advancement for the protection or enhancement of Nature.
- The regulatory system is designed to act as a traffic cop. If it can control a specific violation in a particular locale, it is presumed to be doing its job and, all together, the community is presumed to be better off. That approach does have merit as far as it goes and is better than nothing. *However, it does not have room to look for solutions to problems on a bigger scale. It does not pull back far enough to see that there are vastly superior ways of protecting and enhancing the environment than micromanaging small potential impacts to the land or a creek that are more in harmony with Nature's needs, far less expensive, not confrontive, and provide benefits that are highly predictable.*
- Locally impacted areas are not analyzed in a regional context ... which means larger opportunities are unseen and therefore lost.
- Many agencies within the state and Federal governments have laws giving them access to the regulatory processes. Among them are the U.S. Fish and Wildlife Service, National Marine Fisheries, and the Corps of Engineers, each of which has jurisdiction in some areas. However, no *single* policy applies.
- The offices of the regulatory bodies reside in large cities, and many people who work there have insufficient knowl-

edge of the real-life problems of the affected communities or landowners.
- Judgment-based (rather than science-based) processes have ruled because, in many cases, no real science was available to provide guidance for all involved.
- An inherent distrust exists between landowners and the staffs of agencies—agencies that have the power to withhold approval and produce delays, and lead therefore to much higher costs for landowners—whether individual home builders, developers, businesses, or government agencies.
- The numerous agencies with their numerous gray areas of environmental regulation naturally evolved into a whole new industry, with its associated political power. It was made up of private consultants in many fields such as biology, hydrology, hydraulics, lobbying, legislation, and the law. There were engineering, biological, lobbying, and legal firms dedicated to working in this confrontational regulatory environment. Many developed reputations as successful combatants and were known to lean to one side or the other ... at the same time benefiting, through their billing, from all the confusion. There is now an entire industry working on "environmental protection," and it is complicated beyond belief. We made it that way. It is joined by the advocacy groups, which heightens the complexity and confusion.
- Most advocacy groups started out as small assemblies of dedicated, concerned citizens. Many have been very successful in shining light on special problems. Many, however, have also grown into industries. Over time, self-interest set in. Fund-raising, overhead, and simple survival have become increasingly important goals, even primary goals. They need a crisis du jour to keep donations flowing in. Conflict-based regulatory processes serve them well.

They are politically powerful in representing the causes that interest them.
- The most pressing concern is that the small regulatory wars taking place with applicants cost a lot, are highly contentious, have unpredictable outcomes, and produce a very unsettling effect on land values that does not work in favor of habitat protection.
- The center of control is too remote. Washington is a long way away. That serves the interests of many entrenched participants, since the remoteness create isolation for those in decision-making positions—isolation from the affected fields and the communities—and it places the lobbyists in a position of having clients who will pay for them to carry the message to Washington . . . lobbyists who become de facto experts in the eyes of those in Washington, many of whom are more interested in short-term solutions than embarking on multiyear alternatives.
- The existing system often does not encourage looking at larger land areas to see the benefits of encouraging some impacts in otherwise impacted areas while having those who are benefited contribute financially to expanding other permanently protected areas.
- Local interests have delegated upward their concerns about the environment, to the state and Federal governments . . . and got lost in the resulting bigness . . . in the bigness of the government regulatory bureaucracy. So hot potatoes go to the Federal government . . . which applies Band-Aids . . . which are too costly, insensitive, and remote to do other than what's either politically expedient or is dictated by the staffs. Special interests get results . . . because politics is not a donation of service . . . politics is a *profession*—with a grand retirement plan.

All of these points (and more) keep many proposals that would help the environment from finding the light of day. And all the while, the societal demand for growth—for new housing and new businesses—consumes more and more land and associated natural values.

### *Again—The Bright Light*

Some good news!

As always happens, a few local projects were envisioned that did not fit the normal paradigms ... that seemed sensitive to the environment yet required finding new ways to bend the regulatory format and mind-set.

They were inspired by local initiatives that were desired by individuals, companies, and other groups who had a vision that could not be stifled by bureaucratic rules and regulations. Some, for example, involved permanently setting aside large acreages as habitat for endangered birds; others planned sections of large river valleys and put in place stringent land-use controls based on environmental objectives. Many initiatives found rich soil in which to put down roots and became trendsetters. They became like bright points of light, change-agents. They were to be that. To meet their needs, the required studies were made, the information debated, the conclusions arrived at ... and slowly the rules were bent, as an overall sense of serving a greater good took hold. Not many at first ... maybe a few in each state. But a few.

Each became a *planned response* to man's relationship to Nature, to natural values in a geographical area. Each tended to be comprehensive and deal with all the important environmental values *and* with man's activities. Boundaries were described for those activities, and the involved communities grew accustomed to the effect of the plan on land-use and environmental decisions.

Given the difficulties I outlined above, how did these excellent projects get through? With superhuman effort, commitment, and an untiring interest in working the system to have it make sense. Thank goodness, because they now offer us a clear alternative—if they are embedded in a nurturing national, state, and local program.

Models of excellent local planning are seldom portable—i.e., directly usable elsewhere—because a unique community birthed them and very special interpersonal chemistry was required to make them happen, including shared interests, trust, and commitment. Nevertheless, there were some important fundamentals common to these brave early commitments and we need to take note of them, because they point toward where we are going. We learn two principal things: (1) these models encourage us by acting as guides and (2) they must be developed locally, by local interests.

Finally, there was and still is gravel in the gears of the regulatory approach to environmental management, and yet successes are popping up . . . not as a result of individuals' feeling beholden to complex regulatory principles that lack long-term focus yet nevertheless represent our collective response to environmental concerns . . . but as a result of local excellence having found its way to the surface. That holds the key, as we shall see.

## *GRAVEL IN THE GEARS: A SUMMARY*

- Environmental issues and regulations are being addressed in and by numerous, often conflicting, Federal, state and local agencies.
- There is no regional context, overview, or plan for regulatory actions, therefore no comprehensive vision for long-term management of resources and man's relationship to them.
- Environmental management rests almost entirely on conflict-based policing of land-uses to assure "no-net-loss" of desired resources.
- "No-net-loss" does not encourage or support innovative, regionally important solutions.
- Local government has been removed from participation in important environmental planning decisions.
- The current system consumes important human and financial resources in conflict rather assigning those resources to collaboration around a defined common goal.
- Our environmental management policies lack clearly defined, sustainable objectives for the various environmental regions of the nation.

# II

# WHERE ARE WE?

## *We Have Lost Our Way*

Does it surprise you that we plan highways, airports, computer networks, railroads, sewer systems, hospitals, tax collection, moon shots, and ten thousand other activities that are important to modern civilized life ... and we do not have a national policy for planning a relationship to our nation's environment? The media are quick to report problems with the environment (oil spills, beached whales, landslides, forest fires) ... but when will they, and we, become equally concerned about the long-term relationship we have to the earth?

Do I see protection of the environment as my sole reason for living ... my true and only calling? No! But I am a strong believer in sensible priorities.

I have a lifetime of experience with engineering, public policy, and the environment. I see that the growth of large population centers, the industrialization of much of our agriculture, and our fascination with short-term economic return have left any long-term interest in the environment on the back burner ... the result that we have *no* clear vision ... *no* plan.

Whether we say so out loud or not, we clearly act as though we have dominion over Nature and can get whatever we want from her.

This feeling, which has grown swiftly to match the growth of our modern economy—both the industrialized economy and the information economy—is supported by the fact that we no longer grow food in our backyards and we are remote from our natural support systems; we recognize that we can import foods and raw materials from all over the world if we can't find them here. In fact, large numbers of us have no idea where most of our food comes from anyway or how it is processed. The system is all too complicated and too overwhelming . . . and so we rely on others to take care of us.

However, if we were given a choice, a new path . . . one that plans a long-term relationship with Nature . . . would we even consider it seriously? Might it be worth our while to see if looking at the natural values of our environment on a national level could guide land-use and natural preservation issues for the decades ahead? We would know how all the land would be used and preserved from this larger perspective—in which we can make a deal with Nature called a Master Plan.

Let's first ask some questions and maybe give ourselves some time to think about them . . . considering each one carefully before moving on. The questions include:

- Is it true that regulatory processes have saved the day and are working?
- Is it true that regulatory processes are the only ways to create useful results?
- Is it true that local governments can't be trusted because they are too close the politics of land development?
- Is it true that we have proactive national, state, or local plans for protecting the environment?
- Is it true that we can indefinitely continue the slow attrition of environmental values and assume Nature will not revolt?
- Is it possible that environmental protection and planning—as objectives—have gotten lost in swamps of power and politics?

- Can it be that the time has come to look around and see if our short-sighted, self-serving processes and energy-consuming policies are working ... or if they are just the logical outcome of an out-of-date system that needs to be changed?
- Can it be that current regulations do not encourage flexible solutions to environmental problems? As an alternative, for example, landowners might be encouraged to develop land only within designated areas and could clear their land of environmental restrictions by purchasing and dedicating land for permanent high-value habitat areas elsewhere.
- Can it be that the model we show the world is one of internal conflict and no planning?
- Can it be that after several decades of our needing an environmental regulatory strategy, it is time that even we who are devoutly supportive of the environment need to step back and say we are failing?
- Can it be that something may be learned from the successes that have taken root in spite of existing regulatory systems and their conflicts, and nevertheless have been able to flower?
- Can it be that there is something to be learned about these local initiatives that might be used as seed for other efforts?
- Can it be that creating a centralized regulatory strategy for protecting the environment has led to the development of agencies and organizations that cannot be sensitive to local conditions, are designed to find fault rather than to be creative, are subject to unproductive peer pressure, and avoid the risk of supporting excellence?
- Can it be that the conflict-based regulatory system was necessary but has now served its purposes and can be retired in favor of processes that have demonstrated their ability to encourage excellence at a local level rather than discouraging it?

- Can it be that there is too much government involved to allow fledging environmental practices to take off?
- Can it be that institutions interested in environmental issues do not and cannot afford to shift to a planning-based strategy because many of those involved will face the *inconvenience* of being forced into new ways of life?
- What grade would you give the local, state, and the Federal governments in caring about and being effective in dealing with proactive environmental common sense?

The approach we have been taking to living within our environment reflects our obsession with gathering details without a simultaneous dedication to knowing what we're going to do with the details after we've gathered them . . . trying to solve environmental problems through analysis and ever-deeper science without having an overall picture in our collective minds of what success might look like. Maybe considering Wholeness—a true Master Plan—looked too big, too political, too complex, too intimidating, too daunting, too hard to describe for us to tackle, so we turned our attention to grappling with beloved details and tended to complain about the lack of vision of the whole.

I am reminded about the story of a man, a new resident in his neighborhood, who woke up one morning smelling smoke. He hurried his family to safety in their front yard, grabbing his cell phone on the way out and hitting the speed-dial number for the Fire Department. When the dispatcher answered, the man gave his address but realized he had no idea where the local Fire Department was. With horrific images in his mind of his new house being reduced to ashes before the firefighters could respond, he asked urgently, "How long before you can get here?" The dispatcher said calmly, "Fifteen seconds, sir. We're just around the corner from where you live."

The man, as many of us are, was simply too close to the immediate situation to see and appreciate the whole picture. So, too, with regulations—for we are stuck to a restricted perspective about land-use that prevents us, as a matter of policy, from seeking and finding expansive new solutions as part of our long-term relationship with the earth.

That's why now is the time to take the (perceived) risk of stepping back and seeing the whole ... which is best approached by having Nature's expression of herself in mind and seeking a plan that values that expression... then setting it forth in a national document. The document would clearly designate the lands that are to be preserved for Nature and those that may be put to use for man's purposes.

My job in life as a professional seems to have been to step back ... way back ... so I can catch the greater perspective. I tend to do this naturally, for it is how I am wired, yet anyone can do it by starting with an *intention* to do so. By stepping back farther and farther, we get to a place where we open to something much larger, and through that discovery we find very simple solutions to very complicated issues ... with the further advantage that solutions we find almost always sell themselves and are accepted by others. Why? Because somehow, in being born of a balance that includes the Wholeness that can been seen by stepping back, those solutions *feel* right to others. (My book *The Six Principles of Creative Problem-Solving*, published in 2005 by Juniper Springs Press, discusses in more detail the virtues of stepping back to see the greater whole.)

*Once areas to be preserved or managed for environmental purposes are clearly defined, (whether they will also be used by man or not), the need for "regulation" is gone ... and now the issue becomes just a matter of compliance with the terms of the Master Plan. The result will be clean boundaries between man and Nature that designate the expressions of Nature as paramount. There will be plenty left for man, and it will be of a quality that enhances man's life.*

When the wars over no-net-loss and regulatory efficacy are set aside, there will be much energy available to support the Plan. Read on . . .

## *Attitude Changes: Who Speaks for the Trees?*

Each morning, as my schedule allows, I go to the cafeteria for a cup of tea and a muffin. I usually find someone to sit with, and we normally talk shop. This morning is different, as it will mark an important and radical shift in my professional life.

As I enter the cafeteria, a supervisor from our Construction Division waves me over to a table where he is sitting with a number of his workmates. A newspaper is on the table in front of them. As I approach, the supervisor points to the newspaper, tapping his finger on a very big photograph of several women chaining themselves to large eucalyptus trees. A bold caption reads, "Project Stopped By Protesters."

The supervisor says, "John, can you believe it? We try to protect people from flooding and they're more concerned about saving some damned windbreak trees?"

I'm not certain what he expects from me, but I don't think he gets it. I would have told him what I was thinking if he'd asked. I am, in fact, puzzled.

He continues, "You're the great planner around here. Why wasn't this taken care of? The contractor's going to want a big change-order related to the delays. We stopped the project."

I look more closely at the photo. The women. The chains. Really, though, all I see are the trees. Questions pour through my mind about them. Why are they being cut down? Is there a choice? Who'd made that choice? Can't we save the trees *and* still provide needed flood protection?

Several of the men are looking at me, waiting for an answer.

I say, "I don't know. The city designed this project, and I doubt that anyone here even thought about the trees. I'll check and get back to you."

As I leave the cafeteria, I know something is wrong. I wonder: when the bulldozers and tractors set about their powerful tasks, who speaks for the trees? Doesn't everyone know they are also important? Are they just a zero-value impediment that needs to be cleared and taken home as firewood?

I return to my office and write a note to myself to visit the site, then sit quietly for a few minutes.

The thought of the Los Angeles Flood Control District promoting publicly supported projects without concern for natural values immediately starts to take form and nag me. Something within me sees an important key here, an important fundamental idea or fact or policy or practice that needs my attention, but I'm not quite sure how it can be expressed. I need to get out into that natural setting to find an expanded view.

By late afternoon I can't stand it. I need to act. I cancel my appointments, get in my car, and go to the site.

Looking along the street and seeing the trees suddenly clarifies for me what the key is. The awareness floods into me and I feel that my mind has been opened. I know what needs to be done. Here, the trees are being sacrificed to avoid a short-term disruption of traffic and some repaving costs. In the present world, that is the way it is done.

*However*, I am aware of myself thinking, *a new vision is here.*

It is as simple and as fast as that. In the time it takes for a new idea to be welcomed in a willing mind—which is the thinnest slice of time—I have it. A door has opened. These kinds of things, I recognize, must involve more than just engineering.

In my head it sounds like this: *We must have a voice for environmental values that are affected by our projects. We must also have a voice for community values. These must not be just "least cost" projects. A new balance must be found.*

I can see it as clearly as I can see the street I am standing on. From that day forward, my visions of the District's planning, design, and operations functions include a deep regard for a balance that is needed between humanity and Nature. I know both can be served. I accept the challenge to find institutional ways to change our old practices and add those two other ingredients to the least-cost recipe: "natural values" and "community preference." In one sense, I think, my entire life has brought me to this moment, for the boy who grew up living in and loving the outdoors, who knew and valued the natural world in a way that few people do in this modern world, now has an opportunity to nurture and care for that world in return for what it has given him. A blessing, indeed!

I have seen the key, and now I glimpse how such changes can affect hundreds of public works projects. I will also initiate a series of events, both personally and professionally, that will completely change my life over the next several years.

# III

# A BETTER CHOICE

## *Saying It . . . My New Orleans Manifesto*

*Several years ago, I was invited to attend a national gathering on the environment and to address the assembled conferees on a subject of my choosing. Only a few minutes after receiving the invitation, I knew what I wanted to talk about . . . which was <u>change</u>.*

*What follows here summarizes some important events that preceded my talk, then presents the talk itself, which offered another perspective on the environmental matters I cover in this book.*

I've just entered the conference room of a large hotel in New Orleans. The room is empty now, but in two days I'll be here speaking to several hundred scientists who have gathered for a conference on the environment. Months ago, when this event was in the planning stages and just after I accepted the invitation to speak, the sponsoring organization asked me what my talk would be titled. I knew generally what they wanted from me, and I also knew generally what I wanted to talk about, so without much trouble I came up with a title that would cover anything I needed it to: "The Vision for a New Millennium."

In the intervening weeks, I'd put together a few ideas of what I wanted to discuss and an initial list of some specific points, but I'd not yet come up with a theme I could wrap it all around, a thrust to give it the verve and energy it would need. I wasn't too concerned, though, since I knew I could trust my instincts to bring something through, and I knew my passion would add the necessary enthusiasm to whatever it was. After all, when I draw on decades of personal and professional experience to address an issue about which I feel very strongly—national environmental policy—I am not exactly working in the dark. But I was still a little uneasy about not yet having an overall sense of how I was going to present my ideas.

I had arrived earlier that morning by air from Los Angeles and checked into the hotel. I was looking forward to a free afternoon to do more thinking, more preparation. Lying on the bed, I reviewed local promotional handouts about the city that are provided at the front desk, and I was reminded that the French Quarter is only a short walk away. I grabbed my windbreaker and headed off to be a tourist, happy to forget about the forthcoming presentation, though I did make the brief stop at the conference room to check it out. With that done, I realized I had the rest of this day to play.

As I walk into the French Quarter, I see the names of famous jazz personalities being advertised or memorialized. I see many restaurants and much French architecture, featuring detailed black ironwork. But after a half-hour I'm getting bored, so I turn and walk toward what my map says is the Mississippi River. Any river seems to attract me, and I haven't met the Mississippi before. As I walk, the city street opens onto a large park-like area and the river sweeps abruptly into view. It is enormous, a graceful snake moving from left to right. Beige and tranquil, it suggests a full load of fine sediments and low velocities, nothing like the explosive seasonal rivers of the Southwest.

I buy a hot dog from a vendor and sit on a bench to eat it, enjoying the time alone, the fresh air, and this view of a legendary river I've heard about all of my life. I open my map again. It shows a colorful sign and an arrow directing people to the ferryboat dock. They offer river rides.

I'm drawn to the water.

The ferry is waiting. I buy a ticket for the next tour and step on board, climbing to the top deck and sitting on one of many empty seats up front. The view is perfect. I can look around the dock area ... at the many new office buildings ... across the river to commercial waterfront activities ... and along the river that emerges like magic up ahead, around a bend between buildings. It flows toward us, carrying its beige sediment to add to the deltas downstream.

The weather is clear, breezy enough to enhance the outdoor adventure I am on. I buy a cup of coffee and settle back.

The horn toots to warn the world that the ferry lines are freed, and she pulls away from the dock with a great effort, reflecting the fact that our movement is upstream, against the river's flow.

The dock slowly recedes. I immediately notice that the river actually does flow north in one of its curves—that is, away from its destination in the Gulf. I had imagined that due to its size and force, the river would flow directly and powerfully to the Gulf. Not so. It is ambling toward its destination in response to the flattening slope of the land.

After a short run upstream of a few hundred feet, the ferry turns downstream and the engines are cut back. It is cradled now in the flow of the river and moves as one with it, except for minor turns where they're required.

We pass several historic monuments that are described by the voice from the scratchy loudspeaker near me. I can sense a different era—when our forefathers were settling the area. I tell myself I will return someday and spend time appreciating all they did in that difficult yet simpler time.

In those days, people and the river had a different relationship. People gave her space and found a place of balance where both could coexist. Now, many seek to control and minimize the river's impact, to use all of the "protectable" land for their own needs ... never mind the river's needs. They—we—have lost our connection to the forces of Nature, including rivers, which are a foundation of our life.

We drift downstream for maybe two miles then cross the river and turn upstream once more into the current. The riverboat goes to work again to push its way back upstream. I muse that the riverboat is much like we are. It must now work hard to return to its dock. We must now work hard to relate to natural forces in order to return to our Dock, to a balance with Nature built on mutual respect and conscious interdependence. We must reconsider carefully the assumptions we make about our having dominion over Nature ... especially if we do not fully consider Nature's opinion of our viewpoints and our accompanying actions.

The view of New Orleans with the river cutting right through it is exciting to see. I think of the vast watershed upstream in many states and the inevitability of the flows of the river, locating whatever space they require to find their way downstream.

In front of me I see the levees that protect the city by controlling the river's lateral movement. It is clear that man has estimated her requirements and planned boundaries along her edges. My assumption is that experience in most years shows the space she has been allocated to be satisfactory. But why is anyone surprised when, on occasion, she takes more?

I am looking at the result of a human-developed Master Plan for the river that essentially says, "You, River, can have *this* much space—and we will use the land beyond your banks."

I notice that the buildings in front of me are occupying all of the space adjacent to the river. I wonder if the space there is being shared with the river, or if it's been stolen from the river. If it's the latter, trouble is guaranteed. Why? Because people must coexist with the river, which is Nature, and *Nature dislikes being told what to do.* That is the truth and the reminder from this riverboat ride.

I reflect on my experiences 1700 miles away in the Southwest, where, in the absence of year-round flows, flooding that only occurs every five or ten years led to encroachments into Nature's flood plains. The result was infrequent but large flood losses when the water did come. The key to dealing successfully with that circumstance was a plan, a vision of the relationship of human beings and Nature that served both—a balance where the solution was easily explained, provided reliability, and was adopted into law. It is called Flood Plain Management, and it works.

Suddenly I've got it! That's the answer! That's what I'll talk about day after tomorrow! *The need for a vision—a vision for objectively planning people's interrelationship with Nature now, and not waiting for Nature to make the first move, as she will, and then having to react in pain and panic to her action.*

As the riverboat is tied to the dock, I feel energized by my consciousness of this fundamental belief, supported by repeated experiences—that humanity and Nature must find a better balance. In fact, Nature will demand it, as she should. And yet, we currently see her as our subject, a natural force we have triumphantly overcome and conquered—a terrible miscalculation—rather than a loving Partner who serves us. Nature in a blade of grass continues to grow—to serve—in spite of our repeatedly cutting its top off. But a river we rely on, once severely altered by mismanagement, may not continue to be friendly—to serve—and the battle for control may be escalated. We risk our future when we become out of balance by placing our short-term interests ahead of the long-term need for co-existence.

Rather than planning for and reaching toward a sustainable balance, we seek—incrementally—merely to reduce our immediate impact. To accomplish this, we have built institutions and regulatory programs that strive to minimize further damage, however they lack the vision and planning needed to see the whole—to embrace a long-term objective—and their record of overall or lasting success is, at best, ragged. In fact, I feel those programs are, and therefore we all are, failing unnecessarily.

The next day arrives and I get to breakfast early with a notepad, to see if I can capture a few key thoughts—flashes of light that might catch the attention of this scientific audience. Several ideas come to mind, a few that are products of my lifetime of experience and a few that pop in as a result of yesterday's river ride.

I'm ready!

The time has come to give attention to the conference—to its tone and its issues. I slip in quietly through the rear doors and begin listening to a presentation that is already in progress.

I look around and see many middle-aged men, a few younger men, and a very few young women. These, I realize, are people who can make a difference, however they must be willing to work for change they can trust, drop their current stultifying roles in the regulatory world, and return to implementing the elements of the dreams that brought them to this work with Nature in the first place. Through that rebirth, they can make the most important contribution of their lives—creating a vision and an accompanying plan for the future that respects all life and the Nature they love.

This audience is made up of people who have the time and professional stature to allow them to travel to and participate in this national gathering that deals with environmental policy issues. I am certain they must be feeling internal conflict, for they surely suspect they are the people who can support change and influence others to encourage change . . . and yet they are also the people who, for reasons of personal and professional security, are deeply invested in the current system. Not a comfortable fence to be sitting on.

The room is very large, and I recognize that developing a feeling of intimacy with the audience members will be difficult. I realize that if I want to be *heard* when I speak, I must be as personal, energetic, and direct as I can possibly be. I do want to be heard.

I put away my few breakfast notes and watch the proceedings.

The lunch break comes and goes. I spend it walking in the sunshine and eating a small salad at an outdoor cafe a few blocks from the hotel. These are the times when my ideas coalesce. Various thoughts are now swarming around in the back of my mind, and I know some of them will find their way out of my mouth during my presentation.

I ask myself, *Who am I to be telling this audience of people from across the nation about turning scientific energies at national, state, and local levels toward real goals and plans and long-term environmental success for the nation . . . and for Nature?*

Well, why *not* me? In my career, I have found keys, had visions, solved problems, created regional plans, done what many said could not be done.

I might feel uneasy now, but I don't. I recognize that if I talk cleanly and clearly from my personal experience, from my heart, all will be okay.

When the time comes for me to speak, I am waiting offstage, then the Conference Coordinator introduces me and—there I am in front of them . . . with a head full of ideas that I can already feel are starting to streamline, to take the shape they need—as I begin . . .

I make a few introductory remarks, thanking the appropriate people and organizations, expressing my genuine delight in being here. Then, looking out over the large hall and the hundreds of faces I want to connect with, I hear my own voice.

"I come to you today with a strong message, a heartfelt appeal that we reexamine what we are doing in the response to growing concern for our environment. I have divided my few minutes with you into three segments. They are *Why I feel worthy of speaking to you*, *What concerns me*, and *What I propose doing about those concerns*.

"First, why I feel worthy of speaking to you today. My background includes decades of work in engineering and management, dealing largely with water-related and environmentally critical projects and issues. I have participated directly in the birth of many exciting, state-of-the-art projects as well as regional plans that numerous people—usually for a long list of really good reasons—said could not possibly be developed or carried out. My work has been evenly split between government and private clients, but all of my work has been on large regional projects.

"In preparing to speak to you today, I asked myself—*why did these projects and plans of mine succeed?* One important reason is that behind every one of them has been a carefully crafted plan. Each such plan contained—in thoughts, words, or pictures—details that described my objective in specific terms, that depicted the solution to whatever particular problem, situation or need I had been hired to address. Most have been innovative, outside-the-box, farsighted plans requiring courage—from me and from my clients—to develop and present. Each contained critical natural ingredients, was proactive, and when described was easy to understand. Most were implemented.

"In my experience, a plan is an essential aspect of describing what we *mean* by our dreams and our visions, and it should embody our respect for our partner—Nature. The plan sets forth the specific actions that must be taken over a fixed time, including specific objectives as well as the policies, rules, and the method of implementation.

"Many people do not understand our science, yet they will support a clear, simple plan, an objectified vision . . . and they are comforted by the security it provides, since it speaks to the anticipation of a knowable, secure future for each of them—us—working together with Nature. I can't remember any exciting project I have worked on that did not have a simple, appealing plan that gathered widespread support.

"So I come to you with years of experience in creating and implementing farsighted plans that involve and take into consideration a balance of engineering intentions and Nature's needs.

This brings me to the second segment of what I want to discuss today—*what concerns me.*

"Numerous very successful environmentally sensitive local activities are underway today. They are supported by visions, they carry the energy of cooperation, and they set out to overcome obstacles and conflict with thoughtful solutions. They were created and brought to life without waiting for others either to bless or torpedo them. Several of you participated in these activities, a number of which are well-known. My experience has been that successful local projects or regional planning efforts come about as the result of an unusual nexus of local interest and excitement, even *fervent* interest and excitement, along with perseverance and personal commitment. I have noticed over and over again how *intense* the commitment must be to bring these projects to life. And I have asked myself many times, *why*? Why is it difficult for worthy projects or plans to reach maturity? What are the problems? What changes are required to remove the obstacles for other such projects?

What concerns me? First, our few successes are not nearly enough. Together, they are just a drop in the bucket. Second, in most cases and particularly at the regional and national levels, we have no vision, and we have reached a point of environmental paralysis! We are stuck! We are afraid to act boldly, to define an environmentally sound future, so in most cases we don't act at all. We do not set forth our objectives in plans and build consensus. We would rather see the matter of reaching a regional or national consensus as an undertaking that's too big to handle, then hide in our foxholes, rely on ineffective regulations, and wait for retirement. The conflicts we enter daily in the name of protecting the environment waste time, money, and goodwill. Feeling overwhelmed, we settle for second-rate solutions and hope the problems will go away. As a result, our local and national policies do not contain or support an actionable, balanced plan for long-term environmental success. They embody only a limited environmental policy based on the negatives of regulation, and they embody no pioneering action plans rooted in practical details. It is no wonder we are in trouble, that we are failing in spite of many small local successes, and that our overall policies are virtual prescriptions for failure. Let's look at this more closely."

In this moment of brief, natural pause. I take a sip of water and watch the audience to see if they seem to become more attentive as they await my "closer look" or if they sit unmoving, as though they are bored. I see a few people shift in their chairs. Others don't move at all. But then I realize that gauging audience reaction will not help me. I am not here to please them. I am here to plead a case. Watching to see if they like me will just be distracting. Thus I continue, my resolve back in place.

"We talk a lot about the environment, yet much of what we have done as a nation—as representatives of government, as scientists, as managers, as business owners, and as citizens—is second-rate. This is because we have no clear, long-term objective! We lack the very element I have found is absolutely necessary to success, *a plan based on respect for the greatest good.*

"Many of you, as I do, have some gray hair and are well aware of and frustrated by our nation's lack of success in addressing environmental issues and arranging for a future that is compatible with Nature. We all know that communities say, in poll after poll, they want to protect the environment. I think what they mean is that they want a healthy and attractive place to live, with simultaneous active attention being given to care for and preservation of natural values. Deep down, *most* of us want that. Many of you, in fact, have devoted your lives to work that could lead to those goals, and for that, I salute you. If, however, the citizens of our country really want a balance between people-needs and environmental needs, why are so many of us who work actively with environmental issues so upset about what we are actually doing, about what's actually going on? Why are we paralyzed? In the face of the polls that tell us what people want, what is our response? Do we have one? What is preventing progress?

"Let me ask two questions. The first is: *what's wrong with what we are doing now?* After all, we already *do* have laws to protect the environment. And second: *what can we, based on our experience, recommend as alternatives that will have lasting value?*

"Let's start with the first. The basic framework for our environmental policy today is *protection through regulation.* As such, unfortunately, the policy relies on a system where too many agencies play traffic cop in an endless number of small-scale tug-of-war actions that pit regulators against each other and against a variety of existing or proposed land-uses or activities that are perceived as possibly having negative effects. It is not based on a plan—an objective statement of our dream for the future that truly balances mans' and Nature's needs. It is based on a belief in progress through discipline and control of one interest group by another interest group. That has never been successful in humanity's history—except in totalitarian societies, and even those societies have eventually fallen, because accepting that kind of control is contrary to human nature and ultimately just will not work.

"This regulatory process requires a vast amount of energy and creates enormous friction through confrontation, distrust, and legal action, which most of you here are familiar with. And it seeks to enforce arbitrary types of 'no-net-loss' or 'abide-by-standards' policies.

"Most of us would say it does not encourage or promote cooperative implementation of large-scale visions for long-term environmental balance.

"Nevertheless, we have built huge institutions—government and private—to 'protect the environment' from abuse, and nearly everyone likes that idea. It sounds good, though few people like the results. In addition to the fundamental problem of our relying on regulatory policies, the *survival* of those institutions becomes their own primary interest, even eclipsing their initial charge. Furthermore, many of them also require contentious issues either to excite congressional support or for their fund-raising efforts and membership drives to be successful. To stay alive, they need *problems* more than they do *solutions*."

My attention is caught for a moment by what seem to be murmurs of approval at my statement, which from my perspective is unarguable anyway. I am heartened to hear that they are apparently paying attention. But I have moved beyond approval-seeking now. What's important is what I'm saying.

"Why, for example, would an environmental organization want to find balanced policy-solutions that would actually work for developers and builders—since it needs those people as foes? Its members, seeing this success, would correctly sense that a workable middle-ground had been found and turn their attention and their financial support elsewhere. So the callus of this condition grows and hardens and leads many people to lose faith because they feel there is no solution. There are *many* solutions, however, and we need not despair—except as we look at some of our past behavior.

"These environmental lobbies and organizations have actually caused political interests to *fear* changing current regulatory and conflict-based policies to more proactive visions and national, planning-based solutions. Why? Because the contributors to those organizations think such changes would lead to a radical diminishment of their power and ultimately to the defeat of their influence over legislated public policy. They would lose power! However, if change leads to preservation and to the expansion of environmental values, that 'defeat' would only mean a loss of power for a few, and the environment—Nature—would be served. Even large corporations, whom so many activists regard as the enemy, could be engaged and could turn out to be important allies.

"Certainly those business interests are currently conflicted. Many would like to be seen as environmentally friendly. They spend advertising money to demonstrate their concerns. However, our regulatory system leads to the development of adversarial circumstances that can cause internal managers to find fault with regulatory processes, which seem to many of those managers to lack a viable long-term plan and scientific context and to be unevenly enforced. They therefore tend to engage the supporters of environmental well-being as enemies.

"The current system rewards the gladiators in the battles on both sides and is a sure-fire way to train corporate managers to believe that responding to other than minimum mandatory requirements is bad business policy. Two possible friends—business and Nature—become estranged through the lack of a clear vision and a plan, and we default to the use of ineffective regulation. The focus is negative, not positive—as it might be.

"The result is that the financial energy of corporations does not find its way to the implementation of large-scale environmental plans, because plans they can support without political or regulatory risk don't exist. This is a tragedy! This energy, when it's available through the support of businesses, will be a welcome addition, and all will benefit.

"To recap my concerns, we were on a path based on abuse and distrust, which led to regulation. By using regulation, though, we are falling dangerously short of what we must do to protect and enhance natural communities and our relationship to them. Regulation may have worked for a while, but it is now an out-of-control obstacle. Our challenge is to shake off our paralysis and move on to the creation of a vision, or many visions, and plans throughout the nation, around which we can all rally. My prescription for that follows."

I now give no attention at all to anything outside of myself. The audience, I realize, will do what they will do. I deliberately maintain my focus now on my own inner resources and what I am intent on saying.

"Now, *what do I propose doing about those concerns*? What do I recommend? My answer is to build on what has worked—our successes.

"My experience is that those successes are not random or unique. They have within them the elements that all successes do, and they are not flukes. They are lights we can guide on. They show certain ingredients of success that can be broadly followed and broadly applied. Not to just a few thousand acres but to entire regions or states or even the nation.

"Now what am I talking about? I am talking about having the courage to develop and sustain a vision of successful balance between human beings and Nature—a vision supported by detailed plans. We can create the visions from the building blocks of successful cases in our past work, the ones many of you have heard of or participated in.

"A regional example was the development of a concept for providing Non-Structural Flood Control Systems in Southern California. In this program, we adopted land-use safety standards to keep people safe from the flood-threat rather than trying to contain the threatening flood. Another was the development and adoption of a Natural River Management Concept, which allows a river the room it needs to carry on its natural functions, including erosion, deposition, and vegetation, and yet assures safety for adjacent activities.

"There are numerous examples of regional planning solutions—with which we all, at one time or another, have been involved. In my experience, most have been birthed with great pain from high-energy local projects that survived the regulatory processes. The Lake Mathews project is a pioneering water-quality effort of this type. There, we invented a surface water-quality management system using only natural wetland processes to protect the water supply for 16,000,000 people in Southern California.

"So I ask—why not encourage, foster, and reward the development of these plans everywhere?

"How?

"As part of a bold new approach I propose and call the National Environmental Vision. I ask: why don't we give it a try?

"As part of this Vision, let's let go of the myth that regulation is working.

"As part of this Vision, let's *remove* regulation as the primary tool of environmental well-being and *replace* it with planning.

"As part of this Vision, let's develop and adopt new national, state, and regional pro-planning practices—not as window-dressing, but as clear statements of vision and specific actions.

"As part of this Vision, let's remove conflict as the centerpiece of environmental well-being and replace it with the tools of cooperation.

"As part of this Vision, let's define our environmental objectives in terms of regional watersheds or other naturally identifiable systems.

"As part of this Vision, let's use financial and personal energies to preserve, create, and expand planned environmentally significant areas, and make the process attractive so all can participate.

"As part of this Vision, let's let go of self-interest based on jobs related to regulation or the science that supports it and turn our energy and our future to creating a true legacy for our nation and maybe a model for other nations."

Time for another sip of water and—to be honest with myself—a deep breath of relief, now that all of those things have been said. After a moment, I move on.

"Growth and change will not and cannot be stopped. Recognition of this and of Nature's needs, all built into the Vision, will prevent the continuing tide of regulation and the retreat from real win-win solutions and allow us to step up to protect and enhance the land that supports us all.

"Do we have the courage? Most certainly!

"Is there a choice? I think not!

"That then is my prescription: The National Environmental Vision.

"What is the next step toward creating and implementing such a Vision? How do we retreat from our current rigid stance, squarely address our lack of progress over the last twenty years, and start such a process?

"There are existing models containing the seeds of success that, added to our local experiences, can guide the way. For example, the Federal Emergency Management Agency some years ago was assigned to administer a program to respond to the stalemate over the nation's flood losses. Congress was spending more and more money annually on flood-control measures, yet losses were mounting faster. The conclusion was obvious: there were no effective incentives to stop development in flood-prone areas.

"The program has had many normal start-up problems, yet is becoming effective. Its statements were clear and may carry useful concepts to those of us who are interested in committing our nation and all of its regions to effective, cooperative, environmental planning that can create the needed balance between man and Nature for many generations to come.

"In that program, Congress mandated that each community be accountable for managing its flood plains to reduce or eliminate flood losses through flood-loss reduction plans. The Federal government mapped flood-prone areas. Guidelines were provided. The incentive included subsidized insurance for several years. However, the program is, in most regards, a local program with Federal oversight.

"That program demonstrates how Congress and the President can set in motion the National Environmental Vision using Federal law, Federal guidelines, and Federal seed money. It can concentrate responsibility and accountability at each level of government and avoid interests within and between government agencies that are often competing. It can effect grass-roots activity and, within a few years, birth a permanent program—the National Environmental Vision—setting forth the required long-term environmental values, along with means for their protection and enhancement, in a way that balances the needs of man and Nature.

"From my experience, passing the job to local government, as the Flood Insurance Program does, makes many who are accustomed to local regulatory actions very nervous, yet it can be Federally supervised and it will bring local economic pressure to bear. That is a forceful incentive, and workable solutions will quickly evolve.

"How do you move away from regulatory, conflict-based, institutional rigidity to a new process that will require the environmental landscape to change?

"First, we—you who are listening to me today as well as the greater community of concerned individuals—we see the National Environmental Vision being proactive, expansive, and truly committed to a permanent balance between man and Nature—not block by block, or standard by standard, or bird by bird, but region by region—and altogether, the nation.

"Second, we look at the keys to making it a reality. We ask: what are the critical thoughts and ideas and earlier successes? For example what science is needed, what evaluation processes will be required, and so on? Many good minds are available to seed this process. Once we have the keys in hand, we can gather the tools and incentives available to help at the state and Federal government levels. Tax credits come to mind.

"Third, we develop support for this imaginative initiative and find a spokesperson, a leader, who will bring it forward without fear of the next election. Soon our paralysis will diminish and our job will be to implement the Vision we have created.

"So I invite you to join me in this Vision—the National Environmental Vision—made up of locally developed and implemented regional plans under Federal supervision. These are plans that would need to be formally adopted and look forward many decades.

Many of you in this room would be the fathers and mothers of those regional plans.

"This is an idea that needs to be implemented and can embody the best of our personal experiences over the last twenty years. It can move us all to cooperation rather than to unsuccessful battles. Rather than trying to save a bit of this and a bit of that, we can paint with a bigger brush and see a vision where everyone stands together and contributes his or her energy to a positive, long-term outcome.

"Our nation and our little globe need leadership and a willingness to let go of our old comfort zones and to convert our quiet anger into action that will have durable value and be a model that recognizes the needs of Nature and man, region by region.

"We in this room are in a unique position to support the change. And a leader *will* come forward.

"We cannot wait for population growth to dictate, through the politics of panic and desperation, policies that lead to an ineffective environmental outcome. No one can resist the economic pressure generated by the development of commerce and housing. One by one we lose, because we lack a collective vision and a way to animate positive public support.

"As you leave today, imagine the results fifty years from now of our continuing with existing policies, as compared with the results of our having a clear vision, cooperatively implemented, of the needs of future growth—meaning people—and of the environment—meaning Nature—in a balanced plan, the National Environmental Vision. We daily plan our sewers, phone systems, electricity, and the Internet. Why not elevate the environment, which is the basis of all life, including ours, to the level of every other infrastructure?

"Lack of action will guarantee that we'll look back one day and say, 'We can study the depths of outer space by sending *Explorer* to Mars and we can develop laser-supported surgery, yet we have, in the meantime, misused our environment and missed the opportunity to do something essential for our earthly home, something so simple and so loving—for the world and for ourselves.' We must act before Nature says 'no' to us. We must find balance. And the time is now!

"The National Environmental Vision will not be a heroic undertaking. It represents common sense, and even the most cynical among us knows there is nothing to lose and maybe everything to gain.

"Later, you might stroll over to the Mississippi and contemplate her significance, her natural processes, and all she symbolizes. It is with *her* soul that our private, corporate, and government souls need to reconnect.

"Having no national vision means having no sustainable balance—history has made that clear. So let us commit ourselves to change, and to a National Environmental Vision. And let's add a date as a target and call it the National Environmental Vision—2006.

"We have much to do!

"I am delighted to have been invited here today.

"Thank you!"

I have been so immersed in my own thoughts and feelings that I entirely forget to anticipate any audience reaction. In fact, what I hear at first is nothing—several seconds of utter silence—and as I give attention to that, I suddenly wonder if I have failed. Then several people begin to clap, and others, and still others, and then the applause catches on and grows in volume, working its way past whatever reservations the group had been experiencing. Now I hear the swell of excitement for what it is: a heartfelt expression of enthusiasm by this audience of professionals.

Curiously, though, now that I have said what I came to say, and have done so with the strong energy I believe it deserves, I have no desire at all for the spotlight. I leave the large room, shaking a few hands on my way out, but my wish now is to retrace the several blocks to the river to make my connection again with *her*. I notice that a few people from the conference have come also. Some are looking at me, but most seem to have decided to seek whatever inspiration the river has to offer them.

I look out over her waters as I stand on her bank and I say, "Thank you!"

The shuttles to the airport are as busy as when I arrived a few days ago.

Much has happened in these few days. I have been touched, and I have shared my concerns and solutions. I have offered a call for bravery and change. I am happy to be a voice for her needs. By listening, maybe we can avoid her demands.

She will get our attention one way or another.

She will be served!

## *Stepping Back to See How Nature Works*

Opportunities to develop and apply innovative ideas are everywhere. Almost always, the principal requirement for doing so is that someone have the vision to see beyond business-as-usual. Next, that person must stand up, describe the vision and how it might be achieved, then demonstrate its reasonableness and volunteer to lead. This is especially so if the situation or process has a history of trouble.

An example of this is my company's role in obtaining approval for the development of an important new wetland site. The site involves dozens of acres of new plantings and is very important to one of our clients.

When we start to work on this project, only a few successful new man-made wetlands exist, while quite a number of failures are on record—"failure" in this case meaning that the plantings had not grown to be attractive to the endangered bird species we wanted to support, such as the least Bell's vireo.

From experience, we knew that many plantings at any new wetland die and their intended environmental benefit is not obtained. In our failed project, this history of wetlands plant mortality led us and other design-team members to recommend an alternative strategy, which was to over-plant the site we were developing—placing the trees only six to eight feet apart— then allow natural mortality to thin the trees to a density appropriate to the circumstances of the particular situation, but leaving enough trees alive to meet our needs. That seemed like a good idea. In addition, the site would quickly acquire a pleasing external appearance, as it contained enough young trees with this tighter spacing to have, within months, the "look" of a new, healthy habitat. Federal, state, and local regulatory people all agreed, and we produced a "consensus" planting plan for the site. Young trees were planted in a dense pattern to a specification provided by a biologist. John M. Tettemer and Associates, Ltd., (JMTA) managed the implementation contract.

Once the trees grew in, however, the dense planting strategy showed its weaknesses and we realized that it was deficient. Why? The trees grew and grew, taller and taller—but while we waited for "natural mortality" to have its effect, none of them were dying. And the taller they got, the greater their canopy density became. So no sunlight was reaching the earth. Soon enough, we recognized that they were simply too close together to fully develop their natural shape. They therefore had unusually thin trunks, little foliage below ten feet off the ground, and those excessively dense tops that were all competing for sunlight—and our well-intentioned scheme had produced an unhealthy condition that did not serve the trees or the birds we wanted to attract, nor did it nurture the evolution of the wetland as a whole.

At several meetings regarding that site and with the tremendous advantage of having hindsight available, a number of people criticized us. They told us the site looked like an unproductive orchard and certainly did not replace the natural values we sought to reproduce. And—they were right! Our work had, however, been a useful consensus process and a steppingstone for us all. What became important now was this question: what had we learned and what were we going to do next?

As our new project takes shape, we hold an internal meeting to discuss the project that failed and determine how our experience there can be useful in our present circumstances. I summarize the situation: "The old project had problems because we were all nervous about it, and over-planting seemed a good way to get morality insurance. Unfortunately, most of the trees lived, were unnaturally close, and created a low-productivity wetland. We need a new approach to propose to our client and the regulators—an approach everyone can support."

The time has come for true innovation—not merely reducing or increasing a parameter or a threshold so we can nervously creep toward success. We need to take a step that will clearly vault us out of the assumptions and decisions that produced that failed attempt.

Referring to another project in which JMTA is involved, my son Mark points out a contrast. "Our plantings in Aliso Creek weren't on the same spacing as the other site, and those trees are doing well. They have room to be natural." That's the good news. Now the rest: "The temporary downside to the more natural, open spacing of the plants is the need for patience, since the site, like a natural forest, will not mature for two or three years or more."

But it's not much of a downside. It's just what's natural about the trees.

Suddenly, I ask myself a powerful question: *What is natural about the trees?* Do I know the answer to that?

Abruptly, I realize: *That's it!*

I can see it. What we need is to find out how trees work, how Nature, who created the trees and their needs in the first place, would like us to plant the trees. Who knows better than she does? After we get that information, we can compile everything and write it down in the form of guidelines. A manual, perhaps. *A Planting Manual!* Of course! Now that the idea has come to me, it's obvious. We'll do the practical research and produce a planting manual to guide us—and maybe others—in the creation of wetlands. But it needs to be based on real experience in the real world—not on office ideas. No such manual now exists anywhere that we are aware of.

Mark and I take on the assignment. He gathers information from local nurseries on the size of mature tree specimens of the various trees we want to plant. They are riparian trees, such as arroyo willow, sycamore, and elderberry.

With tape measures and cameras, we spend time in the field at the Aliso Creek site measuring the trunk size and drip-line dimensions of many of the trees. I am excited—for we are using Nature to show us the way. Nature will give us plant-spacing dimensions for each type of tree when we simply measure how much room she uses in a natural setting. A manual starts to come together. And I can tell we're onto something because we're having fun!

During this work we make and document several important observations:

1. Each tree has a natural shape and size that needs much more space than is normally allowed in planting plans.

2. A natural riparian wetland is more than trees. It is also understory—grasses and shrubs—that provides seed and habitat for small wildlife.

3. Birds need edges to fly into so they can nest and hunt. A large, dense mass of trees is of limited use to them, because it has less edge than the same number of trees spread out.

4. In designing a natural riparian forest, adding serpentine corridors between the trees as flyways for the birds is good.

5. Above all, anyone planning to plant trees should think like a tree—"become" a tree, see from personal visualization and experience what the tree needs, and then allow for it. Anyone planning to plant trees should think like a bird—"become" a bird and see from personal visualization and experience what the bird needs and then allow for it.

The first draft of our Planting Manual brings together information and experience that have never been assembled before and recommendations that have never been made before. Why hasn't it ever been done? Maybe just because no one has ever thought of it or been willing to do it. But now the information is available. Nor is it just for us. It is information that developers, planners, and regulators can use on this and other projects.

We send the manual in draft form to the regulatory agencies for comment. For reasons beyond our understanding, we receive no comment. Nevertheless, we are aware that we have created, as we often do, a new standard by which we and our work can henceforth be judged. Maybe we are, once more, ahead of our time.

Despite receiving no feedback, *we* use the draft of our planting manual in our current project. Soon, a consensus is reached among Federal, state, and local regulators, and our planting plans are approved—this time plans that have a sound basis and a high expectation for success. I feel very satisfied with the results of this entire process, as it demonstrates the value of creative thinking, persistence in the face of difficulty, and the ultimate value of vision. I note at the time, "We obtained consensus by listening carefully to concerns, interests, and experiences, and finding proactive answers using natural processes. Nature led the way; we followed and so did project support."

## *Surprising Soul-Mates*

*I am always interested in exploring things—particularly those that seem to interfere with anything close to my heart. Such interference may bring out a certain smallness in any of us . . . until we recognize that it can be neutralized through a simple change of attitude. Instead of hunkering down defensively, we can allow ourselves to see or be led to something larger. What follows is an example of how that happened with me—at a time when the Los Angeles*

*County Flood Control District was being challenged by certain environmental groups.*

Around the late sixties, the so-called "green" or environmental revolution is getting underway and gaining prominence in the public's mind. Groups like the Sierra Club are concerned about how such projects as flood-control facilities being developed by the Los Angeles County Flood Control District, which affect environmental conditions in numerous communities, are being planned. Their concern, of course, fits perfectly with my own, especially as it corresponds to my recent awakening about the need for the District to incorporate environmental and community values into its thinking.

I decide to find out first-hand what the Sierra Club has in mind and, to the surprise of many people, discover after many months of working with the Sierra Club that their proposed solutions to many of the flooding and life- and property-hazard issues the District faces every day are startlingly similar to our own. It even turns out that the chairman of the local Sierra Club and our Chief Engineer, Art Bruington, speak from the same podium to the District's management conference and sound a great deal alike.

Thereafter, I make certain that the work of Project Managers at the Flood Control District includes being aware of the interests of groups like the Sierra Club in regard to projects that are processed within the District. I insist that the Managers take their roles seriously, because they are the only people inside the organization who have specific knowledge about what the outside people want. For their voices to be heard is important.

### *Contrasting Possibilities: Primal Choices*

It may seem strange for certain readers to encounter the view—my view—that it's time for us to make some hard decisions about our environment.

What? After all these years?

Yes! After over two hundred years!

I can't imagine anything more exciting than being able to participate in a decision that could lead in such a different direction for the land in the United States. The decision will affect where we live and work for decades to come, and what our children will inherit from us.

Because we are one of the major political, military, cultural, and creative powers on this planet, decisions we make about the environment will be seen as a reflection of our core values. We are quick to judge the environmental policies of other countries—such as their allowing centuries'-old forests to be burned to gain one year of land-use for field crops—yet we have not addressed simple planning matters about the environment within the United States. Policies implied by our actions include our supporting the continued use of Nature—to develop her, use her up, and populate her—without a plan to include her needs in our overall thinking.

Where might this lead in another fifty or one hundred years? We act as though we are the masters of Nature by taking her for granted, and we further assume that she has no awareness or voice. We need only look again to the recent tsunamis or earthquakes—or to the fact that, around the world, some 30,000 children a day are starving to death—to be sobered out of any arrogant feeling that we are above it all, too wise, or too clever. We happen to be especially blessed . . . and we somehow take it for granted.

The decision I am talking about is between continuing the regulatory approach we now use as our statement about environmental concerns . . . or changing direction and planning our future relationship to the earth we live on and rely on. The regulatory approach focuses narrowly on preventing small losses . . . it has, *by design*, no long-term vision . . . it can't see tomorrow . . . there is no ultimately desired outcome. It is like fighting a war by retreating. The Master Planning approach, on the other hand, seeks local agreement on setting limits to human use of all of our lands and on the preservation or enhancement of natural values.

*Do Nothing*

The preponderant view of those close to our current system is to leave it alone. Why? Because, though it is not perfect, it is understood and we are getting by. *And, I would add, thousands of people are economically connected to the status quo and are dependent on it.*

The recommendation of almost any blue-ribbon committee of government experts and their attached consultants and attorneys is inevitably to make some minor cosmetic adjustments but essentially to leave things as they are. The committee would recommend we continue what we are currently doing. Anything else looks too difficult and would cause changes that the bureaucracies could not control. Few will change willingly. That is true of mid-life experiences in general ... the glorious past is gone, the future is frightening, so we just don't want to move anywhere. We need to be dragged where we must go.

We are, in the meantime, using a good idea whose time has passed. It had its time because it was easy to implement and met the need to put something in place. It was the standard government response ... "Let's police this matter. Get the abuses under control."

We tried the resulting "do-no-harm" approach and called it the desired result. We offered the nation this "do-no-harm" approach as a creative and practical solution for environmental problems, along with assurances that by protecting small, limited areas from impacts, we were getting the job done. That is not and never has been effective ... it is way too small ... too timid an approach for dealing with the effects our energetic society has on natural values.

And yet there certainly is a choice ahead of us. We can decide, through lack of action, to continue using regulatory processes as our key strategy in caring for lands within the United States—the "environment." We can overlook the fact that there are too many agencies involved (think: the defense or the intelligence establishments); there are no forward-looking, actionable objectives; too many special interests; too many negative incentives; no reward for excellence; decision-makers are too isolated from local communities; it's all too expensive; too litigious; too uncertain; and too personality-driven . . .

But there is another path we can incrementally adopt . . .

***Take a Big Step***

*Along this path, we can set a new course in caring for our land. We can choose to be partners with the land by taking note of—and studying—real environmental successes within this country that have occurred over the last few years* in spite *of the regulatory system. We will find that they broke new ground, created excellence in many ways, and attracted enormous community interest and support. They were right!*

Some people will hold up the very evidence I cite and say, "These examples make clear that the current system should remain, for it obviously didn't discourage excellence." That sounds logical, but it doesn't recognize the fact that many of these "excellent examples" were developed and adopted outside the normal rules and *in spite of* the regulations.* *Each was based on backing away from regulatory detail to observe the region from a higher elevation . . . one high enough to see how wise decisions, trade-offs, and courage could be combined to solve many problems—the greatest of which is the protection and often the enhancement of the environment while clearly committing to defining man's uses of the region.* This brave, bold, effective approach is inevitably a uniquely personal local undertaking. It cannot be mass-produced. As a process, it can be encouraged at all levels and become the fabric of a larger plan . . . a national plan. Once a planning process is adopted, the present regulations can be dropped in that particular plan-area in favor of the requirements built into the national plan. We need to change

---

* An example is the permanent preservation of thousands of acres of natural foothill land in Southern California as a site to assure the future of an endangered bird species. This came about through innovative, local, outside-the-box thinking and perseverance. Truly a regional solution.

things, to facilitate a national plan based on individual successes that have been created locally, to meet local environmental and human needs.

We need our nation to be covered by such plans!

*Another way of saying it: these local successes came about because local interests decided to move beyond the once-useful Band-Aid regulatory approach, thereby accepting the fact that local interests have the strength and courage to create community-based plans. Those plans can show unusual respect for the environment and transform conflicts into highly regarded local master plans for extensive areas of land, whole river valleys, and other large regions. What more could we strive for than that people be freed up to create local excellence?*

We will need to face our demons . . . economic and political interests, distrust, and whole industries built to assure continuation of the Fight—the conflict, the strife—and all the while Nature watches and may wonder when we will wake up. There will be pain that most people will not want to confront. There will be reports of problems on this path. Many vested in the current system of conflict and negotiation will fight back.

There is an answer, however . . . which is that we can make a slow, committed transition (as I will shortly describe) and employ all of those who are currently involved so they are turning their efforts toward creating a National Environmental Master Plan.

How exciting!

What needs to be done?

# IV

# THE HIGH ROAD

## *Grounding the Vision—*
## *Having Chosen the High Road*

Todd Bradshaw was enrolled briefly in the UCLA School of Engineering at the same time I was, except he was a year behind me. We both had motorcycles and right before he dropped out of school, we went on a couple of long rides through the nearby hills together. That's when we discovered what we really had in common, which was an appreciation of Nature. He was from the city, and I was apparently the first person he'd ever met who actually grew up in natural surroundings, so he quizzed me endlessly about the things I'd learned from Nature.

When he left UCLA prematurely, I didn't hear from him again ... until forty years later, after he came across my autobiography, *Who Speaks for the Trees?*, and wrote my publisher, who forwarded the inquiry to me.

I gave Todd a call at the number in his letter and after a brief conversation, invited him to lunch at a restaurant at the beach near my home south of Los Angeles.

Over hamburgers and iced tea, he told me those bike rides we took in the hills years earlier and our conversations had changed his life, alerting him to the astonishing depth and diversity of Nature.

He later married a woman he described without embarrassment as a "tree-hugger," had a career with a Federal environmental agency, and had retired several years earlier with the intention of dedicating his senior years to environmental work. Then, he said, his idealism crashed head-on into reality.

Four years with several pro-environment organizations seemed to lead nowhere. There was a lot of talk, a variety of campaigns and protests for and against various things, and endless rounds of fundraising. But nothing ever really seemed to happen. Then he stumbled across my book and was surprised to see that in my professional life I had found a way to support progress and environmentalism at the same time. Somehow, in my life, the war was over. He said he felt I was onto something important and he wanted to know what it was.

"Todd," I said, "I can tell you the same stories you read in my book, but there's something else that may be of interest to you. What if I told you I'm proposing something I'm calling the National Environmental Master Plan? It could reawaken interest throughout this country in our long-term relationship to the environment and define a sustainable balance between man's uses of the land and Nature's needs, community by community."

He laughed. "A Master Plan? Are you kidding? That would require major changes in the way government at all levels takes on environmental issues. There's a whole industry already dedicated to saving the environment, and I doubt they'd go for any kind of real Master Plan. Their entire approach is to keep doing what they've been doing . . . regulating and fighting local environmental fires with 'do-no-harm' policies. Their viewpoint would have to be scuttled."

I was impressed that Todd could see that. "No," I said, "the existing approach will not have to be scuttled. However it will be phased out in favor of unique rules and policies developed as parts of locally-created regional master-plan elements, as such elements are adopted. There will be sort of a transition policy under general

Federal and state supervision, and the policy will certainly encourage the creation of these local plans."

I could tell he was amazed by what I was saying, and I was excited to begin sharing some of my ideas with him. I continued, "There is a new intention to become proactive in defining our future relationship with the land, Nature, the environment. The energy will come from local innovation and can be tailored to local needs. The central government will be the custodian of the resulting mosaic of local plans that, together, will be called the National Environmental Master Plan. We are adding '2006' at the end, so its full name will be 'The National Environmental Master Plan–2006.' It is a sort of patch-quilt approach that will allow existing local plans to be adopted immediately. There will be incentives for the locals to start planning. In fact, one useful model of this kind of local/Federal collaboration is already working—the Federal Flood Insurance Program. What do you think so far?"

"Wow! It's astonishing. You're actually talking about making a difference, which so many of these people who talk big apparently don't really care much about. How far has the thinking gone on this new approach?"

"Meaning?" I ask.

"It would seem that a new organization will be required, or the old guard will prevent any real change. And some fresh guiding thoughts will need to be articulated."

"That's right. There are already programs in place that involve the locals, the states, and the Feds that have been in place for some years. There are useful models that could be copied or used as examples for skeptics."

"So," Todd says, "are you talking about the general guidelines?"

"There's nothing formal yet. But we do know there are people out there who can contribute."

As I respond to Todd, my mind is full of ideas about the basic elements of successful large-scale local planning. The enthusiasm bubbles up inside of me now ... this is exciting ... I feel the way I always do when this kind of enthusiasm takes me over . . . like I'm a kid again.

"There are a number of basic ideas that have helped me through the years." I see and appreciate the expectant look in his eyes. I don't need further encouragement. "Here are a few that are the most important.

"First, the information to be used to make decisions must be based on good science . . . good mapping . . . good resource-evaluation . . . good trade-off information . . . and a clear statement about the environmental objectives for the region."

Todd is wide-eyed. He pulls out a small notebook. "Do you mind if I take few notes?"

"No," I answer. "I'd be flattered."

"So you were saying: good science."

"Yes, and second, we must build in a sustainable balance between man's activities and Nature's long-term needs. 'Long-term' meaning at least twenty years. If in doubt, we will err in favor of Nature.

"Third, those involved locally cannot be prepared to subordinate the needs of the local plan to political considerations, either locally or at the state or Federal levels."

He writes a few notes.

"Fourth, the Plan must be amendable through formal processes. This will allow it to stay viable over time.

"Fifth, of greatest importance, the Plan must be developed from the bottom up . . . that is, the local level must be developed first, without concern for later reviews or sanctions. Then state and Federal involvement can follow."

I pause while he writes faster in his notebook to catch up. "Bottom-up development," he says. "That's good. Subtle, but really important."

"Sixth," I continue, "we need full local participation, particularly by those who are unskilled in the formal planning process that may be used.

"Seventh, we must be sure that any successful plans addressing similar circumstances be fully utilized as guides. No reinventing the wheel each time.

"Eighth, the local plan, once approved, must be adopted into the National Plan as the binding environmental document for the region it includes."

He finishes his note on that point then says, "Wonderful! Protection for the locals they can count on. Extremely important! Go ahead."

"Ninth, retain responsibility for the Plan and its implementation at the local level, where it is part of the very fabric of the community.

"Tenth, assure that the local politicians are fully engaged in and have a feeling of ownership in the Plan throughout all the processes.

"Eleventh, have local plans that currently exist and that meet good standards adopted into the National Plan immediately.

"Twelfth, have a new organization reporting to the President and governor administer the National Plan at the Federal and state levels, respectively."

"Wow," he declares, finishing his note on my final point. "You've really got this all thought out. It's amazing."

I appreciate his compliment—and he is right. I've given a lot of time and attention to developing these essential concepts. In fact, I've been thinking about them over the course of my professional lifetime. Indeed, they are just places to begin and are subject to modification as development proceeds . . . but they are a good start.

"Are you really serious?" Todd asks. "Can this actually be done?"

"Yes, it can. I've seen enough go-nowhere reports written to satisfy lobbyists or big-money interests or to get someone's name on a letterhead and I'm not interested in doing that at all. I don't have time to waste."

"Yes," he says. "That is very clear." He looks at his wristwatch. "I've got to get back now, but I promise you I'll be in touch. This is very exciting!"

As we exchange good-byes, I am thrilled at his excitement, for there's no reason at all that others, upon hearing these ideas, will not be equally enthused.

*A vision being brought to earth! I know how to do that. What a wonderful threshold to be crossing!*

As a nation, we may soon set out on a path of change on which we seek to turn the Vision into a Plan, a real-life, working document that clearly demonstrates our intentions about living with Nature. Not with pitchforks and lawsuits, but using a consensus document we all prepare together. A National Environmental Master Plan.

As we ponder where we've been and where we're headed, we can say:

- A National Environmental Master Plan is long overdue.
- It can eliminate piecemeal, inconsistent, and contentious regulation that has not *created* anything, since it was designed to *prohibit* things.
- We can adopt a model of the planning process we will use to create the Plan.
- We can substitute cooperation for conflict.
- We can step back and see with clarity the best plans for large regional areas or watersheds.
- We can assure full participation of all who are currently engaged in the regulatory processes, including scientists, attorneys, teachers, lobbyists, and regulatory staffs at local, state, and Federal levels.
- We can assure local support by returning planning to the local governments, under Federal guidelines.

## *Preparing Ourselves for Success . . .*
## *The Ten Action Steps*

"We seek to define and reflect in our society, our economy, and in every community throughout the United States a new, permanent relationship between man and Nature."

"Now there," I say to myself, looking at the words I've just written, "is a brave sound bite." I like how it reads, particularly because I know the basic building blocks of what it's referring to will come from local planning, not decrees from a government office thousands of miles away.

Many people are going to ask what it really means . . . it will probably make them nervous, because it sounds different from the old regulatory strategy . . . sounds more idealistic . . . yet it's based on creating and assembling locally developed plans into a national patch-quilt.

In setting out on this commonsense adventure, we must welcome the risk of creating change to reach a new plateau, to move beyond conflict to cooperation, because we will finally have a common environmental objective—to reach higher and attend to natural values that are being challenged by too much growth and too little care. And we may also be creating a model for others.

As we step into this new way of looking at our environment, we will need more than slogans. We'll need layers of new thinking that are put in writing, in plain English, so they can be easily understood and evaluated by everyone. We'll need statements we can discuss and vote up or down. They can be regarded as the core ideas that, when animated, will burst forth into the magic of the Environmental Master Plan.

Below, I have assembled a list of what I call Action Steps, which are the most important steps in actually implementing the Plan. Taken together, they are also one way of representing the core philosophy of the dream.

# Ten Action Steps for
# The National Environmental Master Plan—2006

1. Step back and see through new eyes, a beginner's eyes, the overall benefits of a National Environmental Master Plan, assembled from numerous locally developed regional plans, a bottom-up policy.

2. Seek to have the regional plans serve the greater good of the region, balancing the needs of Nature and the needs of people.

3. Accept that man's activities may be limited where they have the potential to affect natural systems and wildlife.

4. Create, through regional planning activities, plans that identify and clearly define, in physical and legal terms, the land areas and land-use controls that apply to man's activities and Nature's ongoing uses.

5. Remove regulation-based policing strategies in favor of plan-compliance strategies in regions with adopted plans.

6. Establish clearly that Plan development and enforcement will be at the local level. Plan adoption and compliance oversight will be at the state and Federal levels.

7. Assemble the National Plan by starting with qualifying existing regional plans and adding others, over time, until the Plan is complete.

8. Fund initial development of the regional plans using Federal and state start-up funds. Ongoing costs will be provided locally.

9. Replace existing regulations with regional plan-compliance requirements when a region's plan has been adopted.

10. Establish a single office—the Office of Environmental Management—in each state, and at the Federal level, to administer and provide oversight.

## *Rising High Enough to See:*
## *The Las Vegas Inspiration*

*What follows is an experience from my professional career that demonstrated clearly to me how our level of perception affects what we see and how we interpret what we see. Note that what was apparently a small local issue turned, as a result of my taking a higher view, into a result with far greater meaning and far less cost than it might otherwise have had—thanks to a little helicopter and a few gallons of gas.*

### Vision: The View from Above

I'm a few minutes early as I drive my rental car into the North Las Vegas Air Terminal. I see the small helicopter we'll be traveling in this morning, a Hughes two-seater. A sheriff's helicopter. The City Manager of Las Vegas has arranged for this private flight.

The pilot, in his sheriff's department uniform, is also just arriving. We meet next to the sleek little flying machine.

"I'm John Tettemer. Good morning."

He is curt and does not give his name. "Where'll you be going today?"

"I want to look over the whole Las Vegas Valley."

"Any place in particular?"

"No. Just looking around. I'm interested in the lay of the land . . . from Lake Meade—" I gesture toward the east, where the morning sun has just cleared the Sunrise Mountains "—all the way to the mountaintops near Charleston Peak, over there." I wave my hand at the steep, hazy, gray-and-brown terrain, ten miles or so to the west.

He shrugs. This is all in a day's work for him. "You're the boss. Where do you want to start?"

"To the east," I say. Already I have most of the excursion planned in my mind.

"Okay, hop in!" he says, moving toward the pilot's side of the craft.

*I love what I'm doing and I feel great. My whole body is energized—feeling this unbounded freedom to explore natural processes from above, to let Nature's story move into my mind at my own pace as I absorb an overview in sync with my own rhythm. I can, during this special time, create a model of her needs and see options that will stay in my mind for years.*

I open the Plexiglas door and jump in with the energy of a youngster at an amusement park. I hardly need the step, though I do use it.

Once inside, I follow the deputy's lead and buckle the seat belt. I wonder if most of his passengers would play it cool right now, like flying doesn't excite them. I don't know. What I do know is that everything I'm doing today excites me.

He hands me cushioned earphones with a microphone attached. "You'll need these so you can give me directions as we go."

I put them on as his hands move quickly, flipping switches, twisting knobs, making adjustments preparatory to starting our journey. Now the engine comes to life. I am halfway expecting the hammering of a piston engine. Instead I hear the increasing whine of a jet. My eyes follow his to the gauge marked Oil Temperature. We both watch it with particular interest as the needle rises quickly into a green zone.

I am ready. He and the bird are ready. He grasps the collective and advances the throttle with a twist of his left wrist. As the engine noise changes from a steady hum to a high whine, I watch while his right hand goes to the other control—the cyclic, the stick between his knees. The rotor now engages and starts its slow acceleration with the characteristic *whup-whup-whup*.

My excitement continues—high flight in a plastic bubble and an overview of the land I seek to understand. This is my classroom and I love the teacher, Nature.

With his left hand, he changes the rotor's pitch. We lift off with the usual shudder, then three feet above the ground, we rotate in place to face the southeast and our initial destination.

*The acceleration that comes next is, as always, exhilarating. It's a pure body sensation, like suddenly going up a hundred floors in an immensely fast elevator. But the big difference here is that you can see straight out into a wide panorama of nothing but sky and you feel like you're <u>in</u> the sky. This, my body and mind both tell me clearly, is real flying.*

I can see everywhere! The front, sides, and bottom beneath my feet are one continuous, curved plastic window, like I'm suspended in air. I watch the airport drop away below us as we rise and head toward the city of Henderson. I glance at the altimeter—we're already 1500 feet above the floor of Las Vegas Valley. Below us are the buildings of downtown. I identify those facing Fremont Street as well as the curved shape of the large City Hall I have been in many times. We proceed, paralleling Boulder Highway. I have a large map on my knees, unopened. I don't need it yet.

I gesture directly ahead and say into the microphone, "When we get to those big chemical settling ponds in Henderson, go left and follow the green strip over there down to Lake Meade."

"The Wash," says his disembodied voice through my headset. He's reminding me pleasantly enough that he knows this area, that "the green strip over there" is Las Vegas Wash.

After a few minutes, at the appointed place in Henderson, we bank to the left. The morning sun is straight ahead twice—once in the sky and once reflected in shimmering patterns from Lake Meade, about ten miles ahead. We continue eastward, losing altitude to match the drop in the desert below, so we remain the same height above the terrain.

Approaching Lake Meade, we can see its true size: *huge*. It looks to be miles across and disappears out of sight to our left. I see the gray concrete arch of Boulder Dam on our right, holding back the water of the lake. The dam seems too small to be able to restrain the enormous spread of water behind it.

Just ahead I see a small fleet of weekend fishing and sailing boats, neatly tied to their docks in Las Vegas Bay, an embayment of the lake where Las Vegas Wash enters.

The boats are now directly below us, as we cross the shoreline and fly out over the water.

After a few moments, I ask the deputy if he'll make a 180-degree turn and head back to the west, following the Wash.

He nods silently.

I imagine he's usually searching for or following people when he's flying his wonderful machine. Bank robbers, crooks who've stolen cars, suspects in crimes. I likewise imagine my mission today makes little sense to him, since I'm apparently "just flying around." Maybe he thinks I'm a friend of somebody in City Hall. This would help explain his bored-to-death attitude.

We make the turn to the left. A gust of wind from the lake catches us and we bounce a few times, then the little chopper settles down as I return my attention to the vastness of the scenery. With the morning light now at our backs, we have our first view of the entire area to the west—which is what I've come to see. It's startling and impressive.

In the foreground directly under us is dry, barren, rocky, natural beige-and-gray desert that is typical of the Las Vegas area. There is more, however! Cutting through the beige sand and rock, and in stark contrast to it, is once again the rich green swath of Las Vegas Wash—a snakelike oasis along the sides of a small blue-water creek in a ravine some ten to twenty feet deep that ranges anywhere from twenty to fifty feet wide. This natural creek carries flows from hundreds of developed and undeveloped square miles in Las Vegas Valley to the west, just ahead of us. This view adds detail to the first impressions I got from studying a hydrology map before the flight. I love seeing it from up here.

The flows in this once-dry wash are now year-round as a result of growth-driven runoff from the county and city sewage treatment plants being released into the Wash and finding their way to Lake Meade. This new water in the ancient dry channel causes erosion that destabilizes the natural balance of the Wash. Thus, thousands of tons of riverbed material are being carried into Lake Meade as the Wash seeks a new balance. The flows also moisten the soils, which immediately germinates wetland plant seeds that the winds scatter everywhere—seeds looking for opportunities. As the plants have grown, a rich, dense, green streamside jungle has been formed.

The swath below traces a wiggly green line off to the west toward its source in the urban area upstream. We are following it.

As we regain altitude, I see the valley ahead. It's like a big bathtub, with Las Vegas Wash its sole outlet. Nearest us, in that bathtub, is a huge wetland. It is also supported by the flows in Las Vegas Wash. On flatter terrain than the Wash beneath us, it is a gently sloping green plain of arroyo willows, tule, salt cedar, and other wetlands plants that, like the plants in the Wash downstream, flourish in the warm desert sunshine and abundant wastewater from the valley. I can see that the wetlands have filled out to occupy hundreds of acres, an area that I guess is over four miles long and up to several hundred feet wide. It is an oasis for animals and a natural treatment system for stream flows.

Beyond these wetlands, to the west and north, I see the densely built, glittery downtown and the equally famous and extroverted Strip coming into focus—the casinos, showrooms, and attached hotels. This cluster of buildings on Las Vegas Boulevard and Fremont Street is what most visitors associate with the name Las Vegas. These buildings sit in the middle of my area of interest, and though they don't look very big from this altitude, they are of primary concern to the city that brought me to town as its consultant and set me up with this E-ticket flight.

The issue—as these matters often are—is simple. Infrequent, severe thunderstorms migrating north from Mexico can be devastating, and the City Manager has hired me because he wants his city protected from them. Or as I am putting it now: I am here to discover the keys to protecting the bathtub area from damaging floods and to see if practical ways can be found to apply them.

My mind turns briefly to remembered childhood images of a dry creek bed south of Tucson, Arizona, near Nogales. I see them as if it were today. Ongoing thunder and screaming winds and lightning on all sides are nearly overwhelming. The wind-driven rain comes down in sheets of large, swollen drops. I am eleven years old. My Uncle Jack and I are parked on the only part of the road that is well above the adjacent dry creek bed. Our car's windows are open slightly to allow fresh air in.

Within moments, the streambed fifty feet away will be transformed. When we stopped here a few minutes ago it was dry. Then, as if we are watching a Disney spectacular, a wave of water two feet deep, pushing tumbleweeds and small branches ahead of it, comes into view, flowing from our left to our right over the sandy streambed. Just behind it and moving faster is a bigger wave, twice as deep, filling most of the creek bed and eating at the stream banks. Waves of water are now undulating along between the banks, one after another.

The heavy rain and the fog building on the windows mask our view. The waves look deeper. I am nervous, feeling cold and trapped. Could the car wash away if the water overflowed the banks of the streambed? We don't dare get out. The floodwaters are now five or six feet deep in the creek, which is barely staying in its banks. The sky darkens further and all hell breaks loose. What else can happen?

It is midday, yet almost dark. I can smell the free-scented ozone from the lightning. The wave-crests in the creek upstream are now washing across the street nearby, higher than the roadway. I can see that the road has been washed out, as though it weren't even there. The large metal culvert that was under the street to carry flood waters has been torn loose and washed away. It may never be found. My mind can't grasp what is happening. Noise, water pounding on the car's roof, little visibility. The air is thick, wind and lightning continue. The road is now gone.

What's that—over there? It's a huge tree bouncing along in the waves on the surface of the creek like a cork. It is a fresh green tree, maybe twenty feet tall, with colorful green and yellow leaves and a full beard of scraggly roots. It must have been uprooted and washed away as the storm reclaimed the space she needed for her floodwaters by eroding the banks.

My vision improves as the rain suddenly slackens and I can see the tree tilting, twisting, and bucking along as it is washed around the bend in the creek and away from us, out of sight.

Now the rain stops, faster than it came. Suddenly the air is clear and fresh, the sun peeks through, and I see patches of blue sky.

The violent storm cell leaves as rapidly as it came.

We start the car and drive on, in the direction the tree was going. The road this way is untouched.

I think about that storm for days. I remember reading a sentence somewhere that has stuck in my mind: "The desert thunderstorm gathers strength quickly and challenges anything in its path."

I understand that better now. My instinctive youthful thought is, "Be prepared. Either stay well away, or learn her ways well." I make the conscious decision to learn her ways.

Now in the present again, flying above the Nevada desert, I call on my awareness that the damage from a major flood can last for years. Nature in her intensity is truly amazing. I am reminded that a flash flood can float cars, destroy homes or businesses, and wash away people and livestock in minutes.

And why do I care? Because protecting people from flooding is what I do. It is my life. It is a solemn charge, but also a game—one in which I need the clearest vision possible, because she has awesome power. And I have fun trying to anticipate her moves and accommodate her needs.

From inside the plastic bubble, my eyes shift past the center of Las Vegas to the area beyond the flat landform of the valley, to the vast undeveloped areas of sand, gravel, and rock between the valley floor and the mountains to the west. These areas have distinct shapes that reflect how they were made. We are close enough that I can see the pattern.

Below each of the distant mountain canyons, I see the distinctive cone shape of sand and gravel and rocks that have been washed from the mountains in thunderstorms and deposited on the flatter slopes of the valley below. The material comes naturally to rest in the form of a fan, radiating from each canyon mouth. The larger material comes to rest first and closest to the mountains; the finer materials are carried downstream and deposited in the fan or cone shape I am looking at.

I say aloud, "Every mountain canyon has a cone."

The pilot looks at me quizzically, wondering if I'm talking to myself or him.

I say it again, "Every mountain canyon, like those over there, has a cone-shaped deposit."

He nods, catching on now that I am talking to myself, not to him.

This is a key, one of several! From up here, it is clear how the cone's shape forces the discharges from the mountains to spread out as sheet-flows across a wide area of the cone. This pattern of spreading makes predicting the exact path of flood flows in any storm very difficult. By contrast, the flows of the Colorado River behind us enter the river and can't wander. Everyone knows where they will be: in the canyon bottom. Below us, however, it is only clear that the flows spread. There is no stable riverbed. It is an alluvial plain, sometimes called an alluvial fan. A very different animal. I remember seeing these cones from the air in Utah, Arizona, and California. And now in Nevada.

I make a note on my pad: "*Cones.*"

I know they will play a role in my recommendations.

We continue west—as the town passes underneath. In my headset, I hear some chatter between the pilot and an air traffic controller. Probably about permission to be flying near the traffic of McCarran International Airport. I don't pay any attention.

We start to climb, following the topography up and to the west, above the unpredictability of the alluvial cones. Directly under my feet I can see the gullies that cut into the cones, and I can see where those gullies have meandered over time in response to flash floods. The flows and their paths are unstable, as the flows can break out and carve new gullies and thus move their points of discharge by miles. They are also very dangerous, because their actions are unpredictable.

I am seeing it all in my mind now, in order, from top to bottom—rugged mountains, alluvial cones, the valley, flood plains, the Wash, and Lake Meade. All in a space of forty-five linear miles.

In the valley floor and cutting across the natural flow paths is the congested development of Las Vegas, sited as it is in the flattest, most flood-prone area of the watershed. From this altitude, the keys are apparent, as are some possible solutions.

I take a deep breath as if to internalize Nature's story. A spontaneous flash of gratitude appears in my mind. *Thank you!* I make a point of not saying it out loud, for the deputy almost certainly would not understand his passenger, the out-of-town Somebody, speaking his gratitude to Nature.

I lean forward to break my reverie and bring myself back to the unfolding scenic drama outside as we head up the cones and continue our climb. Our little bird shivers several times as it passes through convection currents from the desert below. We are nearing the mountains.

I never think of desert areas like Las Vegas and Palm Springs as neighbors to high-elevation, snow-clad mountains, and yet there they are—beautiful, crisp, white snow hats on the mountain peaks to our right. I look at my map and confirm that the highest of them, which is well above us, is Charleston Peak, elevation 11,918 feet. These are the headwaters. These mountains are like Mount San Jacinto above Palm Springs, California—some trees and snowcapped, though just a short distance from the hot, arid valley floor. I am exhilarated by the change from the valley floor to the partially wooded area here in the mountains. I am feeling the changes that birds in flight enjoy. We are a bird in flight.

We lift through 4000 feet to 5000 and then to 6000. I look over my shoulder. Amazingly, we are only about twenty miles from downtown Las Vegas. The cockpit air is much cooler. We are directly over the Red Rock Canyon area.

The tallest mountains are steep, very colorful, rocky, and in some places almost vertical.

This, as I am well aware, is a great place for infrequent floods to start. As rainfall becomes runoff, it is drawn by gravity . . . crashing down the impervious, rocky face of these mountains, sweeping with it anything that will move. The flows thunder down, sounding like a herd of locomotives, often carrying car-sized rocks all the way to the alluvial plains below. Each storm adds its share, makes its contribution. The flows then proceed, colored beige by the soil of the desert, onto the populated valley floor below. I now have the total picture in my mind.

We have been in the air for about an hour when I say, "That's it. Thanks. Great trip. I got just what I needed."

The deputy-pilot nods. In my side vision, I see him watching me for just a moment longer than he probably needs to.

We turn east again, in the direction of the large lake on the far horizon, and slowly coast downhill toward the North Las Vegas Air Terminal.

On the return flight, I summarize my thoughts about my first aerial survey of the whole area. Water rushing down the steep rocky mountains carries anything loose with it. As these flows reach the foothills, the rocks and gravel and sand drop out. The alluvial cone forms and the streams wander around the cones as they wish. From there, the water joins other runoff from lower elevations and, going downstream, finds its way invariably into all of the low, flat areas of the valley floor. There it slows or ponds and floods streets and businesses.

I recall news clippings showing flooding affecting highways, underpasses, parking lots, and buildings near popular casinos. The flows then, very slowly, maybe over several days, drain through the densely developed urban areas into Las Vegas Wash, through the wetland plain, and then down the final descent into Lake Meade. Yes, I have flown it all—I have it all!

I put my pad down on my windbreaker, sit back, and soak up the final view of the valley.

I see the entire Las Vegas Valley clearly. I feel complete. I have what I came for. It is an indelible picture, and I have the keys. Our flight again is rocked by the waves of heat rising from the desert below.

From this elevation and before I return to earth, I put together a synthesis and an overview, a systems view, a complete mental snapshot, a clear image of possible alternatives that will stay with me forever. The names of people and places may fade with time, but the images will not. They will be as fresh in twenty years as they are today.

These images are the foundation of my work. They—not abstractions or principles of flow or theories about weather patterns—are what I see when I discuss problems and options. I see them as I develop detailed alternatives. I see them in public presentations. I see them as an expert witness. They are present at times when I make passionate presentations or offer defenses of ideas. The only requirement for me to grasp Nature's story is to be elevated above the detail—literally and figuratively. She paints with a big brush.

As we continue our descent, I remember talking with several clients about very large-scale projects, each involving thousands of acres of land. In each case they were insistent on telling me what their problems were and what the solution was likely to be. They wanted *my* assistance to reach *their* solution.

As I matured in the role of a consultant, I learned to ask that new clients speak only of their general concerns until I finished my elevated review. I learned to say, "Please don't tell me your objective until I have time alone on the property." I learned to say, "The most valuable consulting time you may ever get from me is the first few hours after I have had my personal time with the land."

My insights come from time with the land. The general options become clear then, as do the probable restraints. The keys are all there. In addition, sometimes a vision, the germ of the answer, may come forward. I have seen the land, the natural images, and can later use them to test many solutions or combinations of solutions. The data is in my head. No numbers yet. Just keys, visions, and images.

Now we are on a straight path to the airport. I can see it ahead, beneath our feet. The pilot says some words into his microphone. I can't make them out. Apparently they are routine. The reply is equally undecipherable, though I hear a few words like *temperature* and *dew-point* and *wind* and *runway*. We cross Rancho Drive and settle the remaining twenty or so feet toward the dusty gravel of the landing site. Rotor-blown dust rises up to greet us. With a minor bump we are on the ground again.

As the rotor slows I unsnap my seatbelt, remove the headset, and gather my briefcase, notepad, maps, and windbreaker. I step out carefully and stretch.

The pilot also gets out, walks directly to the rear of the cabin area, and opens an outside hatch. First my eyes follow him and then my body does. I like machinery.

This activity seems to be a standard procedure for him, starting no doubt with *first get safely on the ground*. Then *check the oil*—or whatever it is he's checking.

I join him—and gasp. There it is, the engine. It is *tiny*.

The pilot explains in response to my obvious amazement, "It's a turbine engine, smaller than the engine in a VW. Weighs just over 150 pounds." Suddenly I realize that this rather curt deputy probably loves to talk about his helicopter.

In that way, perhaps we are alike. I can easily romanticize what I see before me: *This wonderful little device, fed with fuel, had lifted the two of us into the sky, above the city, above the noise and restricted views, to an elevation near the mountaintops where vision was possible. Where the wholeness is available and can be seen. Where Nature reveals herself and where the areas of wet and dry and steep and flat are all evident. The elevation opens the door to information, and through this experience the model in my mind is now three-dimensional and includes possible solutions. This little machine has taken me to a place where Nature speaks to me, where I am far enough away to see her as a whole.*

I silently thank the machine! I have already thanked Nature.

I shake hands with the pilot. "I appreciate it."

He holds up a finger to say "just a minute" and walks to the cabin. He returns with his log. "What's your name again?"

I spell it slowly.

He says, "Thanks."

I walk to my rental nearby.

I'm back in the real world of noise and traffic. It somehow smells different. After a minute I find a break in the traffic on Rancho Road and start toward town. I spot a coffee shop. I have two interests there, one more urgent than the other, and I pull in.

After the restroom, I buy a cup of coffee and a donut and stroll back to the car.

I open the windows and sit back in the seat with my pad and my nourishment. The warm desert breeze has started. It is gentle and comforting. and I like being alone. I slowly print the following between sips of the lukewarm coffee:

> *The keys are: Thunderstorms. Alluvial cones. Obstructed flood plains. Large scale. Not much crosstown flood-control hardware. Arid community ideas. Limited funding. The Wild West.*

Each key is a form of shorthand, a sort of tree-with-branches that I have decorated with my ideas and insights. Each key tells me its own story about opportunities that lie ahead. The way the keys are assembled is what makes the solutions interesting, adventuresome, and sometimes innovative.

I will use the keys. They will be within a vision and later a model of a solution. At this point, I don't talk to others about the keys or the vision, though. They are mine.

On my way to town I notice the buildings getting progressively larger and closer together—more direction signs—more traffic and trucking. This is the current nature of the center of many communities. What seems important to most people is huddled together near the Civic Center.

I have just been above it—with an unlimited view. Now I am in it—with a very limited view. I understand that the scope and openness of my thought is directly related to how far I can see. And conversely, how far I can see is directly related to the scope and openness of my thought. For me, small rooms and small vistas mean small thoughts, while large rooms and large vistas mean large thoughts and the chance for a unique vision, a new way to juggle the keys.

When I am on the ground I can see freely to the local horizon, be it a stretch of land, a building, or a hedge of trees. That is a restricted view. From above I can see the entirety, the vista that shows issues and answers.

I turn onto I-15 South, headed to McCarran International Airport.

It is well-known, if not always put into actual practice, that one can only find solutions to problems by moving away from them to a larger perspective. A problem on a city-block level, for example, may not seem solvable until one sees many blocks at once.

The helicopter flight removed me from the input of others to be alone, removed me from the obstacles and details to see and sense into the bigger picture. That seems natural and has always been my way. Get quiet, open to the larger view, and the critical aspects of possible solutions—the keys—become apparent. How can one find solutions while one is yet in the downtown area of obstructed views? My job now is to use the keys to develop concepts for solutions—solutions that I know, from those keys, will work and are compatible with Nature.

I follow the Rental Car Return signs at McCarran. I surrender my car uneventfully and arrive at the gate just in time to hear the boarding call for my flight to Los Angeles. Once aboard and buckled in, I fall asleep.

### *Concept: The Vision Brought to Earth*

Two days later, I call my five key staff members together to discuss the Las Vegas project. It is to be an informal, half-day affair in our San Gabriel offices.

I open with a summary statement. "The Las Vegas City Manager wants our help with ideas about managing their floods. It's a major problem, mostly because the city has developed in the valley floor, where the flood plains are and the flood threat is the greatest. Runoff from big thunderstorms moves right through town on its way to Lake Meade. Recent storms there have made it a big issue with the public.

"Day before yesterday I flew the area and took a few notes. I understand you have collected some of the available hydrologic and hydraulic information, so let's start."

We settle into a general discussion to see if we can find concepts, some grouping of keys, for study.

Archie Vance, the senior engineer who has worked with me for many years, starts our session. He's the man I depend on to transform my general visions and outlines of models into everyday reality. He says, "The flooding that's bothering much of the city comes from the west and north, where you flew. There are some natural channels, yet much of the flow can arrive from the alluvial cones and is spread out and hard to collect and control. Even if we were to collect it, there are no serious drains we could use to carry it past the flood-prone areas and over to Las Vegas Wash. At first glance, hardly any land is available for building a cross-town drain, besides which creating one in a major street would be very expensive and disruptive."

Alan Swanson, also a senior engineer, who takes the general concepts and makes them work in engineering terms, speaks next. "I've made some calls to old friends in Clark County, and no one seems to be doing much flood-control work in the Las Vegas area. We may be on our own. It seems that floods are too infrequent to get much attention, and the local people are attending to land-development problems, such as new highways and sewers—not regional flooding solutions."

Nothing new about that. I often find we are alone at the front of the line—since that's the sort of work we take on.

I reenter. "If there's no existing major drainage capacity across the city and the practical problems of building a cross-town flood-control channel make that approach unreasonable, what choices or concepts are available?" I tell them that I remember cases where flood-peak retarding concepts were studied by our company and by others. Would those work? What might be their strengths and weaknesses?

I expand on this option. "The congestion of buildings downtown seems to point toward two choices—one traditional, one not. The first, we've already looked at. The city and the county could build large channels in city streets in the urban areas. They would have to be very large, since the slopes, hydraulically, are relatively flat. They would also be extremely expensive and disruptive to build.

"The second choice, my preference after flying over the land," ...and this is a verbalization of my vision ... "is to prevent the large volume of water from getting into town in the first place, to prevent the flood before it can start. What speaks most loudly to me is detaining the flood flows north and west of the congested areas and trying to use existing small formal drains—if any are available—to empty the detention facility when those drains are not in use, following the floods."

I conclude in the most elementary possible terms. "No water . . . no flooding."

Simple enough. The images are clear.

I suggest that we do some preliminary calculations on several different concepts and get together in a few weeks.

In a month I am back in Las Vegas, in the curved City Hall talking to the City Manager.

"I'm excited about the possibilities here," I tell him, with some pleasure. "It appears that we can stop worrying about flooding downtown if we interrupt the flood flows up on the alluvial cone several miles west of town. The floodwaters won't even reach the valley floor." I repeat my simple formulation. "No water ... no flooding."

"How would it work?" he asks, obviously impressed.

I put a three-foot by four-foot graphic on the wall. Its sketches show the area to the west, and our idea of a place there where water can be stored. I see the City Manager's face light up when he recognizes that area.

I say, "If we can collect the flood waters and store them in a large basin, they won't be available to flood the downtown area. The only problem is, we'll need to find a way to drain that basin before the next storm arrives.

"So, with your permission, we want to see if there's an already-existing, developer-built drain nearby that discharges flows into Las Vegas Wash, one we could use during an actual storm when it's not needed for local flows. It also might need to flow for several days after a storm. Everyone wins if no new drain needs to be built across the city."

The City Manager is clearly delighted, and even before I hear his words I know his decision is made.

"Let's take the next steps," he says, then authorizes me to estimate both concepts and also to see if the detention option can meet the technical and legal requirements.

Now he moves from merely giving me an okay to actively accepting his leadership role. I can hear the excitement in his voice. "While you're doing that, I'll discuss getting funds from Clark County, from the fund-sharing program they have with us."

"Great!" I respond, appreciating his enthusiasm.

Then as I prepare to leave his fifth-floor office, he speaks up brightly with something he's clearly pleased to suggest. "You know that basin you'll need to have west of town to store the water in?"

"Yes."

"There's a place that might be perfect for it. It's called Angel Park, except it's not really a park—yet. Right now it's just undeveloped desert land around five miles west of downtown, but it was given to the city for us to turn into a recreational facility. There's even a new development nearby that has some small drains that may help you."

I leave the curved building and walk into the strong desert sun, aware of the Manager's courage in supporting the novel idea that flooding a few blocks away might be managed by constructing a basin several miles out of town. His willingness to step forward for this proposal sets him apart from many others, who cannot see that far and are more comfortable with familiar solutions, such as those that allow floodwaters to collect in the community—which means there is a major flood—after which various channels carry away the entire flood peak. I wonder if the innovative alternate strategy I have proposed, in which floodwater is stored for later release at low rates, will be a hard sell for him. I'd like to think it won't be. In the past, the cost, lack of available land, and infrequency of flooding have delayed implementing downtown solutions. So when storms arrive—which they do—and several main streets have turned into rivers and cars are up to their windows in water, both everyday people and business interests ask urgently, "Why don't we have a program to stop this?" Now they'll have a program.

I hear the sound of running water. It is the city's fountain. I sit next to it and jot down my questions while they are fresh on my mind. This list will be the agenda for the staff meeting when I get back to the office. The questions on my pad are:

*Are there adequate, existing cross-town drains to empty the basin?*

*Is the Angel Park property the city owns large enough and is it properly oriented?*

*Could the portion of the park used for the basin also be used for recreation during the normal, non-storm times?*

*How can we reach up on the cone and capture the elusive water?*

*Might a basin reduce the Federal Flood Insurance premiums being paid by some homeowners and businesses that are subject to flooding?*

*How can we balance basin size, available flood runoff, downstream protection, and the full use of the existing local drain?*

*How does the cost of the basin concept compare with a channel concept?*

I add as a footnote: *The technical-feasibility work needed now is to answer these questions and any others that arise, and compare the two concepts without emotion.*

I put my notes away and set off again for home with excitement in my heart. I hail a taxi for the twenty-minute ride to the airport. A short flight and an evening at home are ahead.

The next morning I am the first to open the San Gabriel office. I want to get started.

With coffee in hand, I gather my team and we go to work. I hand out copies of the questions I have written. Archie and Alan make their own notes as the lists and work assignments become more technical. Two hours later we are done.

At every step and in every individual discussion, I rely on the keys and the vision of detention I recorded in that rental as I drank coffee. They bring me a long perspective in small rooms and assure me that our thoughts are part of a larger system we understand. The keys never change, and the vision will finally turn into a solid idea, a model.

The concept that soon becomes the frontrunner among us is, indeed, to use a portion of the city's Angel Park for a detention facility and then connect it to an existing small local storm drain that will convey the water downstream into larger drains in Las Vegas that eventually outlet into Las Vegas Wash and Lake Meade. Part of its appeal is the city's ability to undertake the project without control from others.

The next step is to obtain consensus.

### *Consensus: A Natural Result*

I know that providing flood protection by using a portion of the city's park not only has support from the city but also its active sponsorship. The City Manager wants it to happen, wants the two uses—flood control and recreation—to coexist. He asks me to develop a graphic presentation that shows how the property can be used, and then to coordinate carefully with his park planner.

My San Gabriel office staff works for several months and determines the basic requirements for the flood-control basin. I envision a big open hole dug into the surface of the desert, much like pictures we have seen of open-pit mining. In this case, channels will collect the flood runoff and direct it to the pit. Due to the need to store a lot of floodwater, the pit may be a mile long and several hundred feet wide. An outlet and at least one emergency spillway will also be required.

Developing this basic concept is the necessary starting point, and now I can push to soften its appearance and blend it with other uses. After several sessions with the city's park planners, we develop preliminary graphics reflecting a balanced use of the park for both recreation and flood control—just what the City Manager hoped could happen.

We complete the graphics. I put them in a carrying tube that fits under my arm, then I'm off to Las Vegas, where I present the material to the City Manager. "I think we've handled everything," I explain. "These graphics show the basin—it's over 5,000 feet long—stretched across the alluvial cone adjacent to Durango Drive, from south of Westcliff Drive all the way north to Vegas Boulevard." I point out that this long, sausage-shaped hole lies parallel to the sloping contours of the desert and maximizes the storage capacity while minimizing the excavation costs. After storms, it can empty into an existing drain downstream, so there will be no need to build large new drains, as some people in town want to do. Also it fits into the park planner's ideas for a golf course.

"I think it's a winner," I tell him.

"I do, too," he says confidently. I can almost see him proudly presenting this graphic to others.

"What are the next steps?" he asks.

I think for a minute. "We just need funding, and once again to identify any possible stumbling blocks." I ask if he's aware of any opposition.

"There's none," he says. "The Council and the community members I've talked to strongly support the idea." Then, moving into his usual energetic leadership posture, he says, "I'll meet immediately with the County about using our allocation of flood-control funds and see if they have any concerns."

As he stands, heading toward his next meeting with a councilman down the hall, he thanks me. We agree that I will stay in touch as I develop the details.

I enter the elevator outside of his office, feeling very satisfied. I reflect with pride on the recent months.

*From a helicopter vision of Nature and the possibilities for protecting the public, to finding a basin, a piece of the vision that has instant support; to finding the available land in a city park; to successful dual-use concepts; and now on to the hard technical work of preparing formal studies, plans, and specifications; and then finally to construction. We have the needed consensus. It fell in our lap, as it often has. What a wonder it all has been.*

### *Implementation: Making It Happen*

Meetings with the County are held at policy and technical levels. We work with the State of Nevada Dam Safety staff. Green lights are turned on everywhere, though those approvals are subject to the customary plan-development and review procedures that inevitably follow.

An innovative regional flood-control project is being birthed in Clark County that will almost certainly be used as a model for flood control elsewhere. The Las Vegas solution will directly benefit the city and it sets the stage for a regional Master Plan using flood-peak detention that affects the entire watershed, well beyond the city limits.

Several years later I am in Las Vegas dealing with other matters. A heavy rain has just fallen. In some spare time, I drive to Angel Park to see my old friend in action. It is nearly full! The water in the huge basin is water that isn't flooding homes and businesses downtown.

To my utter amazement, that afternoon on my car radio at commuting time, a traffic reporter with helicopter noise in the background says, "I'm over the Angel Park Basin."

I can't believe my ears! Someone is reporting on our project!

He continues, "The Basin is almost full, but no water is spilling at this time. I'll check back later."

*From a helicopter vision to a helicopter update—perfect and unexpected.*

My eyes cloud over with tears as I feel the pride of accomplishment. The Basin is a news story now, an active part of the community, seen as an asset that is "doing its job of protecting the city." (More recently I have heard that some twenty more detention facilities are now in the Las Vegas valley.)

I shiver with pride at having been involved. Some part of me is there with this project and always will be.

## *Adopting the Model*

No, I haven't forgotten . . .

We need now to discuss what I have so far been describing as an effective *existing model* that can be used for reference as we create and then set in motion the National Environmental Master Plan. This existing model deals with issues that are similar to those addressed by the Environmental Master Plan, for it involves natural processes and the need to determine—based on precisely identifying particular characteristics of various lands—whether human use of those lands is permitted, or is not permitted, or a middle-ground is permitted under specified conditions.

This existing model, as I have previously noted, is the Federal Flood Insurance Program of the Federal Emergency Management Agency. It is in operation now . . . and is several years old!

It's an exciting program because it is already understood by the Federal and state governments and local governments throughout the United States.

It uses local knowledge by making primary responsibility for developing its technical aspects a responsibility of local governments . . . i.e., the cities.

It places responsibility for its implementation and administration at the local level.

And finally, the Federal and state roles are primarily those of oversight—to see that the program is implemented as planned.

In all, it is a program that has as its basic tenet the cooperation of the several levels of government, led by local interests that are closest to the decision-making involved in land-use.

The Flood Insurance Program has all the features we are looking for . . . not to be used verbatim . . . but as a model of a working government program that deals with technical issues of land-use and natural events . . . a model that can be tailored for use in developing and operating the National Environmental Master Plan.

Among its virtues:
- The program delegates responsibility to local professionals working in local government.
- The program allows decisions, including trade-offs, to be made at local levels as long as they respond to the strict requirements of the program.
- The program came about by representing the best thinking of many experts in local, state, and Federal governments on how to successfully address sensitive land-based decisions.
- The program has attracted many highly qualified professionals to develop and implement it. Local skills have been called upon to administer it.

- The program is old enough to have gone through growing pains from which much can be learned.

Will we hear comments deriding that program as a model? Of course! Part of our culture today is to attack anything that threatens ... when we are fearful, we strike out. We strike out because we are afraid, and our fear is about loss. We strike out with the hope that we can hang onto what we have.

It can be anticipated that some people—reacting to their fear—will actually create stories on the thinnest of evidence to stir up media disturbances about the dangers that lie ahead. You can hear it now ... "The Flood Insurance Program doesn't work because of *this*, because of *that*, and because of *this and that* ... and certainly it is not a useful model. It would lead to locals playing fast and loose with natural values, and species-protection would be lost!"

Those are entertaining sound bites for the fearful, but they don't affect the fact that *change must come*. And how better than by using proven models? Such models are very important, because most people in our nation will understand and support using them if the models can demonstrate that honest progress has been made to craft a new relationship with Nature ... a relationship developed at a local level where people can look the process in the eyeball because they or their neighbors are involved.

In terms of details, there are numerous technical differences between the Flood Insurance Program and the National Environmental Master Plan. But of primary importance is what we can learn and have learned from the Flood Insurance Program and how we can avoid the kinds of problems it may have encountered.

The glass is more than half-full! And the model is useful, since it broke fresh ground by establishing new relationships between local, state, and Federal agencies that, for many decades, had been moving toward the accumulation of power in Federal agencies. A movement in the opposite direction was appropriate, since the flexibility that is desirable for finding innovative ways to meet community and environmental needs is best left with local government, with general Federal supervision.

Under the National Environmental Master Plan, those who have been attached to the concept of environmental protection through regulation will find themselves working across the nation for communities where the real action is, as mothers and fathers of the new National Plan. A very exciting future is ahead for anyone interested in true innovation and real environmental protection.

I hope you join in!

It could be the most exciting and fulfilling time of your life, and of lasting benefit!

## Master Planning an Entire Community

*Here's a much different kind of project that was extremely complicated—starting from basics that included a lot more than conventional environmental considerations. Unfortunately, it was never implemented because the Indian tribe that was central to the project got restless about the effect of this level of development on its property. Nevertheless, the proposal I put forth was extraordinary, one of the most interesting and satisfying planning efforts I was ever involved with. And it illustrates something about the fascinating complexities and benefits of Master Planning.*

This situation, in Arizona, involved the portion of the Papago Indian Reservation that lies adjacent to the city of Tucson. I had previously worked for the same client, a land developer in Palm Springs, on several projects in that California community, and he had learned first-hand of my ability to manage complex projects and of my expertise with water-related issues. He therefore asked me to manage the planning and design team for the Papago project and also to create its flood-control system, using JMTA staff.

Our client had signed leases with many of the Indian owners of this portion of the reservation. The leases would allow him to jointly develop, with the Indians, a complete community that could provide enormous revenues to the Papago Nation. The bulk of that Nation was over forty miles away, to the west of Kit Peak. But because this piece of property was so much a part of the Tucson area, the owner thought it could become a major commercial outlet for the Papago Nation, similar to the way Hong Kong has become a commercial outlet for much of China.

I managed the whole design team of several firms that specialized in land development and matters such as planning, sewer and water systems, surveying, solid waste, and biology. Many subconsultants were involved, though JMTA put it all together, along with a planner named Tim Wilkes. One of the highlights for me was the negotiation with the Indians that was required, since Indian law and non-Indian law are very different, and both needed to be considered in regard to the complex issues of governance, including such concerns as land-use planning, sewer systems, and parks. We needed to find a way to recognize Indian sovereignty while allowing the non-Indians to invest safely in the development of the property. I developed a form of government that was modeled on a county-level system, which had power-sharing between non-Indian and Indian leaders. It got very elaborate and was described in several volumes of text I wrote and negotiated on behalf of my client.

My excitement and major commitment to this unusual work was based on a deep understanding of county government, a strong feeling about the need for balance between non-Indians and Indians, and an appreciation for the Indians' connection to the land and fear of non-Indian dominance.

The elders of the tribe listened to the younger tribe members, however, who said they wanted to keep the property for deer and rabbits and not develop it—and so it was not developed.

# V

# GETTING SPECIFIC

## *Recruiting a Leader*

A National Environmental Master Plan? Of course! How else will we know where we're going?

It makes sense, so how do we get started?

We describe, as I have, the sticking points, why change is required, the needs to be addressed, and a simple solution involving new uses of time-tested ideas, including how to rearrange our current policies and practices to better serve man and the environment by creating a comprehensive vision and putting it on paper.

We then can see a time a few years from now when we will have a Master Plan made up of regionally developed increments; when we will have, through this process, fully engaged every community in decision-making and reawakened them to the important environmental concerns in their regions.

As we proceed, we must recognize that environmental management is fundamentally the domain of government and political processes are therefore involved. We must also recall that management of the environment is entrusted to government at many levels . . . local, regional, state, and Federal . . . and is widely diffused.

We must also recall that each of the public agencies involved has administrators and elected or appointed officials who see environmental issues as hot potatoes . . . making decisions about them is a tough balancing act, influenced by a labyrinth of organizations, special interests, and reams of requirements.

We must remember that few will welcome the change, yet change must come! We will upset the delicate status quo but only for a short while, then reestablish balance as the regional objectives for the environment are adopted into the Plan.

Leadership will be up to a politician or politicians. . . they alone create and can modify public policy. The first step then is to encourage one or many elected public officials across the country to step forward and declare themselves in favor of a locally developed, nationally administered Environmental Master Plan. To begin, only one or two such people will be needed . . . to step forward and describe the vision. More are certain to follow . . .

All who do step forward will need to be resolute in their support and desire to lead, as they will be under severe pressure to leave things alone. They will be told by their staffs, advisors, and advocacy groups . . . "don't rock the boat."

But it is just that responsible boat-rocking I am advocating.

What then are the characteristics we need in these political leaders?

They will need to see:
- The benefits of long-term, comprehensive environmental planning through the development of a Master Plan that will define man's relationship to Nature and Nature's needs;
- The benefits of local participation in each region of the nation in the development and administration of regional increments of the Plan;
- The benefits of consolidating the responsibility for the management of environmental matters within all levels of government;
- The benefits of replacing the current confrontational approach to environmental management with a collaborative effort to develop and administer the Master Plan;

- The benefit of engaging all of those currently involved with environmental management in the development of the Master Plan; and
- Their own ability to stand as agents for change.

How will they be found or come forward?

I believe that when this new vision is clearly seen by those who are attracted to it, they will raise their hands. They will make themselves known. As this process unfolds, several leaders— such as state governors or officials in the national administration—will become the initial focus points. And, due to the requirements that must be met for passing or modifying Federal laws, this initiative will need the energetic advocacy of other leaders at the highest levels in Washington.

The leaders will come forward!

## *Applying the Model . . . Preparing for Action*

We have now recruited a leader, and an initial meeting is convened so we can begin discussing what's ahead. All of those invited this morning are pleasantly anxious, as though they are gathered expectantly in a hospital delivery room . . . knowing something worthwhile is about to be born. They can feel it.

Everyone present rises as the Boss steps briskly into the room. At his side, matching him stride for stride, is his Executive Assistant, Mary, a woman well-known for getting things done and for her rich background with both environmental issues and Washington . . . she's also known for being tough and fair.

The Boss gestures for Mary and the others to sit down. He remains on his feet, living up immediately to his reputation as a man who wastes no time getting to the point.

"We all know each other and can dispense with the formalities, except that I want to note the presence of my Executive Assistant,

Mary, and remind you that she speaks for me . . . her presence on this assignment will signal to you all my intent and commitment.

"This is a very different and exciting day." He speaks clearly and informally. "It is different because I don't normally get involved with environmental issues. Somehow, the government staffs don't think I *need* to be involved, or maybe they don't want my philosophies reflected into regulatory systems that are scattered over the plethora of agencies that often seem to feel as though they, themselves, own and operate the environment.

"But I am not here to discuss the past, beyond acknowledging that it used to be what was happening. It's not anymore, though, because today we are going to start mapping out the initial steps on a new path to our national management of environmental issues. I have read the briefing papers and talked to some senior staffers. I am ready to go."

The Boss rolls up his sleeves and moves from his point of entry into the room around the conference table, then stands next to an empty chair.

"This is an introductory meeting only, but it is very important, because it is the forum I've chosen to bring you and Mary together to develop and adopt our working vision of a very important initiative to which I have already and enthusiastically agreed in principle. Today we're just going to glimpse what's ahead, rather than dealing with too many details.

"But before I turn the meeting over to Mary—"

As he says that, several of those around the table look up in surprise.

The Boss grins and continues, "Oh, I guess I forgot to mention." He gestures across the table to his assistant, indicating that she should rise. As she does, he says, "I want to you to know that all of you—under Mary's leadership—are now involved in the exceptional and challenging task of being my brain-trust to develop and implement the first-ever National Environmental Master Plan."

Mary smiles. Those around the table smile back and nod, as if to acknowledge her and their commitment to her and to the job ahead.

The Boss continues, "And just to make it interesting, I've told her I want the beginning steps of the Master Plan up and running in 2006. To that end, I have placed my full confidence in her. I support her one-hundred percent, and she will have full access to me whenever she chooses. That is how important I think your work is . . . and will be. Now . . . Mary . . . the floor is yours."

Mary looks very comfortable and confident as the Boss sits down. From knowing Washington extremely well, she recognizes that she has just received an extraordinary endorsement. And probably of more importance, all of Washington will know it in a few days when the Boss and Mary, side by side, announce this initiative to the press.

She opens her informal remarks. "This meeting time will be well-spent if we scan the work ahead. I will have it recorded on those flip charts" . . . she points toward the front of the room . . . "and use the input as my initial guide to prepare for the dozens of meeting that will follow, both here and across the country, as we kick off the process of reducing *visions* to a practical *realities* in each community.

"We are sure that Nature, and our relationship with her, will be served—and so will our children, who often are forgotten in today's present-only oriented society.

"We know this initiative is very, very important. We are committed. You can trust that. We also know we will hear many who are close to the existing system saying it will never work . . . and on and on. We have heard it all before, but we must just stand up and advocate what we believe in. Most political bodies across the nation will eventually be involved, so we want to be out in front, urging them from the beginning to join in rather than trying to push them from behind later on. It will make their jobs easier—and ours."

She backs away from the table and walks to the front of the room, where the three large flip charts have been set up. She gives a high-sign to two junior staffers who have quietly entered the room.

"Enough from me for now. Let's start and look ahead, doing so in tiers, one tier at a time. The three tiers, one on each flip chart, will be *Ideas and Issues, Early Action Ideas and Issues,* and *Technical Items.* Pat and T.J. from my office will be getting everything down on the charts. Later it will all be transcribed and distributed. So please speak clearly for them. If they miss something you say, I've asked them to request that you repeat it."

Those in attendance stir and open their own papers in preparation for contributing to this baptismal event. At first, their energy seems restrained, but within several minutes they get a feeling for the flow of things, stimulated by Mary's enthusiasm as she strides around the room asking leading questions, making comments, and offering encouragement.

Before long the flip charts are filling with the ideas from the group about what is ahead. All recognize that the lists are clearly not yet complete or even entirely accurate. All, however, see them as an obviously productive starting place.

A few issues are raised and discussed but further questions are discouraged in an attempt to let the information flow without internal challenge, at least initially. Vigorous internal discussion will follow, Mary affirms, when she has laid out her pathway for the planning—and before the Washington bureaucracies are engaged.

Then, after less then thirty minutes, several pages of the first chart are filled.

*Tier One—Ideas and Issues*
1. *Draft the Plan*
2. *Describe the required science*
3. *Assign responsibilities*
4. *Develop a schedule*
5. *Create required legislation*

6. Acquire models of excellence
7. Maintain Federal oversight
8. Require patch-quilt development at local level
9. Inventory, publish, and rely on models of current successes as the basic building blocks of the Plan
10. Bring current successes into the Plan immediately to start the patch-quilt
11. Create an Environmental Secretary in the President's cabinet and consolidate all national environmental interests under that one department.
12. Establish technical teams in each state using existing Federal and state employees as the technical resources to serve local governments as requested.
13. Establish a national schedule for:
    a. Organizing
    b. Compiling and publishing success stories using the states' technical teams
    c. Develop local plans
    d. Integrate local plans into National Plan
    e. Systematically remove existing regulations and replace them with operation and maintenance policies built into the local plans as they are adopted.
14. Publish progress reports quarterly.
15. Establish an appeal hierarchy process of locals to state teams to Federal Teams.

Mary says, "This is a wonderful start and, as we all imagined, there is a lot to think about. *All* of these items are important."

The Boss says, "I didn't fail to notice the idea of establishing a Cabinet-level post of Environmental Secretary, someone who would report directly to me and have the clout to work with all the Federal agencies involved with the environment. That's a bold step. And I love it!"

In a tone reflecting his obvious amusement, he adds, "I noticed a number of years ago that once this nation started its focus on the environment, every Federal agency set up an environmental section. We were suddenly—and still are—inundated with people who are 'saving the environment' . . . it is a wonder, if those numbers count, that we even have anything left to do here today. But, I don't think I need to emphasize the fact that while we've made some progress, we have a lot more—a *lot* more—yet ahead of us. We've barely begun."

A senior member of the group offers, "Our national situation with the environment isn't much different from that of the military establishment and the intelligence community—areas involving policy, funding, and action that also are extraordinarily complex—where we have likewise been struggling. Each of them is too fragmented and dances to its own drummers, which usually consist of, or are heavily influenced by, constituents who benefit financially from the fragmentation. To avoid that, I think we would be very wise to centralize all of our national environmental programs under one office. It would then get real and be far more responsive. It could be the seat of the National Environmental Master Plan. And by the way . . . I support attaching the year: 2006. That tells the world we expect to see real progress. Very good!"

The Boss says, "I'll look into that carefully. I like the idea. If we care, why don't we act like it? We all have been in Washington long enough to know the answer to that. However, I *do* care."

Checking the wall clock, Mary says, "Okay, good work. Let's finish getting the rest of the tiers on the charts."

Before long, the following items appear:

### *Tier Two—Early Action Ideas and Issues*
1. Confer with those who put Flood Insurance together
2. Assemble Federal start-up team (Mary plus ?)
3. Gather professionals at Fed, state, and local levels.
4. Draft legislation

5. Public statements
6. Assemble state start-up teams
7. Draft the Plan
8. Assign responsibilities
9. Develop a Master Schedule
10. Describe the required science

"That's enough," she says. "Let's see now if we can add some of the more technical items we will want to address. We have just a few minutes, though much more time is being put on the Boss's calendar, starting next week. Okay? Tier three."

### *Tier Three—Technical Items*
1. *Accumulate success stories for many areas and why they worked*
2. *Identify National Parks and other Federal land such as BLM Land*
3. *Investigate role of mitigation banks*
4. *Identify existing preserves and government-owned land*
5. *Assemble list of useful natural solutions, such as the Natural River Management system*
6. *Define trade-off techniques*
7. *Tax incentives?*
8. *Find excellent model of local watershed planning and other regional planning successes*
9. *Clearly identify values to be protected and the land required from regional, state, and national standpoints.*
10. *Describe how local one-stop-shopping has worked for possible adoption*
11. *Consider how to best gather and publish existing national successes stories*
12. *How do we build a file of land-use decisions, or should the locals manage it?*
13. *Create clear definitions of what constitutes compliance*

14. How would Federal oversight work?
15. Define state oversight of local planning and compliance
16. Use Fed flood insurance model to plan development, enforcement, and oversight
17. How to give seed money to states and locals
18. Create a National Environmental Database to list existing successes immediately and to add more successes as they become available
19. Find out what the states need and have to offer to this process
20. Use the patch-quilt idea . . . woodsy and accurate.

Mary takes a breath and moves to the head of the table.

"Again, thank you . . . that's enough for now. I'll get all this transcribed and emailed to you in a couple of days. We will meet again next week and start assigning responsibilities within our own group. It is important that we portray this process and our commitment correctly."

The Boss stands up, underscoring his departing comment: "I want this to happen on my shift," he says emphatically. "I am not in a hurry. But I *am* resolute. We won't push hard to eliminate the existing regulations until we have quality options in place. And when we do, we will transfer the operation to locals just the way the Insurance Program does, even as we retain Federal oversight. I am also not naïve . . . there will be opposition, because the establishment is being challenged . . . well, maybe not just challenged . . . but also fundamentally *changed*."

"And," concludes Mary, "we all know how Washington loves challenge and change. Thanks to each of you for being here."

# A Final Word or Two

## *An Initial Thought*

I feel very good and stand tall as I conclude my presentation to a group of community leaders who gather regularly to discuss local current events. One of its members had read my book *The Six Principles of Creative Problem-Solving* and invited me to discuss it and how it might be applied to working on the Environmental Master Plan.

I don't take many speaking engagements . . . but this one is special, about a subject that has been close to me and my life's work . . . that of finding opportunities to blend man's desires and Nature's needs in practical, caring ways.

In my work, I somehow have been guided creatively to find thoughts that, once brought into the light of day and blended with physical facts, bloom into innovative, applied visions. They look so simple—and usually are—yet initially, like any idea that needs to be recognized before it can emerge, they seem hidden behind a veil that must be parted.

Parting veils is something I seem to be good at. It's one of the things I do well.

Among the simple, exciting, parting-the-veil ideas that have come to me is this: to relax the fear-based regulatory processes we have used to reduce abuses to the environment, then substitute locally-created regional plans that proactively embrace and define the needs of both man and Nature.

Today I have been speaking about just that, about converting a vision, a peek behind the veil, into a true contribution to the quality of our lives and our children's lives, in harmony with Nature.

Too bold? I think not . . . because someone must lead.

Today, here, that is for me to do.

In concluding my talk, I say, "This idea I'm presenting is about taking advantage of the occasions of documented success that have led to excellent, local Master Planning activities and applying them to other areas, until a patch-quilt of quality, locally-developed regional plans is in place everywhere. Those regional plans, when brought together, will collectively take form as the National Environmental Master Plan, built from the bottom up . . . from workable, proven foundations that include a clear definition of these four basic elements: what we choose to preserve, what we seek to protect, what we will utilize, and for what purposes.

"Needless to say . . . institutions that now tend to be mired in self-interest, short-term visions, and limited legislative authority will be key players in the creation of the Plan. But first, that fear-based system will, out of necessity, be replaced over a period of several years with cooperative plans. I believe those plans, because of their overall, self-evident sense of rightness, will be magnetic and attract strong support. I also believe they will clearly demonstrate the benefits of collaborative long-term planning in our relationship with Nature, of locally developed regional plans, and of restructuring the institutions involved.

"Further, and of great importance, major steps will be taken toward honoring and respecting our hostess . . . Mother Earth . . . doing so region by region, with plans that are sensitive to her local conditions and needs.

"Why now?

"Because the benefits of the regulatory method are all used up. That approach is way too small!

"And so, in closing, I recommend that we each commit ourselves to considering the overwhelming benefits of a National Environmental Master Plan—a network of locally developed and supported plans, already proved through experience to be successful, that are then assembled into the national patch-quilt.

"Thank you."

I turn and nod to the moderator, indicating that I am finished with my formal remarks. Then, after a few words of appreciation to me, he announces that I have agreed to take a questions.

A man in the middle of the audience stands up. "Mr. Tettemer, I'm Charlie Williams. I'm a consultant and I work with wetlands. We've met before at various forums, particularly when you were presenting your very ambitious plans for creating wetlands . . . which, by the way, are now mature and a wonderful contribution to our community. But this new plan of yours is . . . well, frankly, I think you're a dreamer—and I think what I've heard today is a dream, a pie-in-the-sky idea . . . an Environmental Master Plan at the national level. It's way too much."

He takes a deep breath, shaking his head woefully. "Everyone—all of the parties—the individuals and the groups that could make your dream come true are right now eyeing each other through slits in their fortress walls. Working with this environmental territory is what they *do*. It's their livelihood . . . and none of them want the kind of change you're proposing. They've built whole institutions to defend their positions and the financial structures they've set up. Those fortresses are manned with dedicated constituents and donors, and are protected by well-paid attorneys. No matter who's in the fortresses—business interests, landowners, farmers, urban environmentalists, or government—at all levels they're hunkered down . . . with their slogans, mottos, pamphlets, and fundraising campaigns. And lots of attorneys. Few of those fortresses, I fear, will welcome you and lower their drawbridges.

"And so," he concludes, with an attitude of obvious, passionate, predetermined defeat, "in the face of all of that, what are you actually suggesting?"

"Simply," I respond, "that we acknowledge that something else has already demonstrated its worth . . . something that has been, and is even now, working in complicated local settings all over the United States . . . that has created versions of the patches in the patch-quilt . . . that has created excellent regional plans. These are examples that, when added together with many new ones we create, will make up an Environmental Master Plan for the nation . . . it's that simple."

Still standing, he responds, "But is that dream of yours big enough, important enough, attractive enough to bring down the fortress walls?"

"*Yes!*" I reply emphatically. "*Yes*. Because it is not just my dream. It is a dream we all share, and one we must bring into reality. It is our personal and collective dream and has been for years . . . all that's missing has been the vision . . . but not any more!

"It is therefore time to act."

### *A Further Thought*

The National Environmental Master Plan–2006 . . . as you are reading this book, can you envision a copy of the Plan resting on your desk? Can you believe in the benefits to us all and to Nature as a consequence of our caring enough for this earth to define how we will relate to it . . . where we will protect it from any inappropriate impact . . . where we will farm it . . . where we will build cities and where we won't . . . where environmental limits will constrain our behavior?

I can.

I am acutely aware that Nature is the larger force on this planet we ride on. The planet *is* Nature. And she will be served.

Our task is to consider how much longer we are willing to ignore our interdependent relationship with Nature and, by doing that, run the growing risk of pushing our environment too far . . . and, to our detriment, forcing Nature to push back. Caring for this home of ours is within our power ... our job is to see the trends just well enough to take reasonable, responsible actions.

I cannot think of a more important next step than saying we intend to plan our use of natural resources through a collaborative process, built from the bottom up, where each community is empowered to define its environmental balances and tradeoffs, and then to adopt specific, binding plans that meet general Federal guidelines.

Pulling back the veil once again, I ask that we revisit the central thoughts, the initial elements of the Vision I first presented as part of my speech in New Orleans:

"Why not encourage, foster, and reward the development of these plans everywhere?

"How?

"As part of a bold new approach I propose and call the National Environmental Vision. I ask: why don't we give it a try?

"As part of this Vision, let's let go of the myth that regulation is working.

"As part of this Vision, let's *remove* regulation as the primary tool of environmental well-being and *replace* it with planning.

"As part of this Vision, let's develop and adopt new national, state, and regional pro-planning practices—not as window-dressing, but as clear statements of vision and specific actions.

"As part of this Vision, let's remove conflict as the centerpiece of environmental well-being and replace it with the tools of cooperation.

"As part of this Vision, let's define our environmental objectives in terms of regional watersheds or other naturally identifiable systems.

"As part of this Vision, let's use financial and personal energies to preserve, create, and expand planned environmentally significant areas, and make the process attractive so all can participate.

"As part of this Vision, let's let go of self-interest based on jobs related to regulation or the science that supports it and turn our energy and our future to creating a true legacy for our nation and maybe a model for other nations."

We need to return to fundamentals . . . once again opening our hearts to Nature and to our own future . . . to reconnect with this aspect of our Source . . . and through our planning, support her support of us.

# Epilog

With pure joy in my heart, I reflect on a note I received today about Irvine Ranch Water District's Natural Treatment System. This system is designed for the natural treatment of urban runoff before it reaches the Upper Newport Bay in Orange County . . . a major environmental asset of coastal Southern California. Of greatest importance to me is that the system was conceived as a *regional* system, for which there was no existing model, and trailblazing was required. I was asked to guide its development.

The note I received says the system—the first regional water-quality management system for the treatment of urban runoff in the State of California—has been approved.

This is the type of local excellence that can, when encouraged, become one of the patches in the National Environmental Master Plan–2006.

## ABOUT THE AUTHOR

John Tettemer grew up in the rustic Santa Monica Mountains of Southern California, a natural setting that deeply affected his life. At age 13 he was sent to a boarding school thirty miles away, where he worked full-time for his tuition and prepared for college. There he met Susan Cronyn, who became his high-school sweetheart and later his wife, lifelong partner, and mother of their four children.

Upon graduation from the UCLA School of Engineering, John was hired by the Los Angeles County Flood Control District. There, during a rapid rise through management ranks, he distinguished himself as a creative, results-oriented maverick and change-agent who was highly regarded for his innovative approaches to difficult engineering and administrative tasks, and for his special attention to environmentally sensitive issues. After 24 years, he had reached the level of Acting Chief Deputy Engineer.

Seeking new horizons, he left the Flood Control District to become president of John M. Tettemer and Associates, Ltd., an engineering firm he founded and subsequently led for two decades. There he acquired a reputation for innovative, often state-of-the-art approaches to large-scale engineering challenges, including flood control, water-quality, and environmental projects. Government agencies and private clients throughout the southwestern United States sought his services.

In his professional career, John became widely-known for his flair for creative problem-solving and his dedication to the environment, as he discovered and implemented solutions that involved complex, multidimensional undertakings—always seeking to balance the needs of clients with attention to the needs of Nature.

Of his unusual visionary approach to dealing with engineering problems, he says, "I've been called a dreamer . . . and I suppose I am." Then he adds, "But I'm a dreamer who gets results."

A detailed account of John Tettemer's unusual life appears in his autobiography *Who Speaks for the Trees?* (Juniper Springs Press, 2005).

CANADIAN MEDICAL LIVES

# DR. ALAN BROWN
## Portrait of a Tyrant

*A.B. Kingsmill*

Series Editor: T.P. Morley

Associated Medical Services, Inc.
and
Fitzhenry & Whiteside
1995

Copyright © Associated Medical Services Incorporated/The Hannah Institute for the History of Medicine, 1995

Fitzhenry & Whiteside
195 Allstate Parkway
Markham, Ontario L3R 4T8

All rights reserved. No part of this publication may be reproduced, stored in a retrieval system, or transmitted in any form or by any means, electronic, mechanical, photocopying, recording, or otherwise, except brief passages for purposes of review, without the prior permission of Fitzhenry & Whiteside.

Jacket design: Arne Roosman
Copy Editor: Frank English
Typesetting: Jay Tee Graphics Ltd.
Printing and Binding: Best Book Manufacturers Inc., Louiseville, Quebec, Canada

Fitzhenry & Whiteside wishes to acknowledge the generous assistance and ongoing support of **The Book Publishing Industry Development Programme** of the **Department of Communications, The Canada Council**, and **The Ontario Arts Council**.

Care has been taken to trace the ownership of copyright material used in the text, including the illustrations. The author and publisher welcome any information enabling them to rectify any reference or credit in subsequent editions.

### Canadian Cataloguing in Publication Data

Kingsmill, Allison Bristol, 1923–
  Alan Brown : portrait of a tyrant

(Canadian medical lives : no. 18)
Co-published by Associated Medical Services, Inc.
Includes bibliographical references and index.
ISBN 1-55041-165-9

1. Brown, Alan, 1887–1960. 2. Paediatrics – Canada.
3. Paediatricians – Canada – Biography.
I. Associated Medical Services, Inc. II. Title.
III. Series.

RJ43.B76K5 1995        618.92'00092        C95-930269-7

# CANADIAN MEDICAL LIVES SERIES

The story of the Hannah Institute for the History of Medicine has been told by John B. Neilson and G.R. Paterson in *Associated Medical Services Incorporated: A History* (1987). Dr. Donald R. Wilson, President of AMS, and the Board of Directors decided that the Institute should produce this series of biographies as one of its undertakings.

The first ten biographies have now been published and can be obtained through the retail book trade or from Dundurn Press Ltd., 2181 Queen Street East, Suite 301, Toronto, Canada, M4E 1E5, and Dundurn Distribution, 73 Lime Walk, Headington, Oxford, England, OX3 7AD. The second group, of which this is the fifth volume, can also be obtained through retail book stores or from the publisher, Fitzhenry & Whiteside.

A.B. Kingsmill's portrait is a collage of Alan Brown's strengths and weaknesses collected from those who were close to him: family, colleagues and patients. It is an objective picture seen through many eyes from different angles and the appearance, to understate it, is not always the same.

There is no shortage of meritorious subjects. Willing and capable authors are harder to acquire. The Institute is therefore deeply grateful to authors who have committed their time and skill to the series.

T.P. Morley
Series Editor
1995

# CANADIAN MEDICAL LIVES SERIES

**Dundurn Press:**

*Duncan Graham* by Robert B. Kerr and Douglas Waugh

*Bill Mustard* by Marilyn Dunlop

*Joe Doupe* by Terence Moore

*Clarence Hincks* by Charles G. Roland

*Francis A.C. Scrimger, V.C.* by Suzanne Kingsmill

*Emily Stowe* by Mary Beacock Fryer

*R.G. Ferguson* by Stuart Houston

*Harold Griffith* by Richard Bodman and Deirdre Gillies

*Earle P. Scarlett* by F.W. Musselwhite

*Maude Abbott* by Douglas Waugh

**Fitzhenry & Whiteside:**

*William Boyd* by Ian Carr

*J.C. Boileau Grant* by Clayton Robinson

*R.M. Bucke* by Peter A. Rechnitzer

*William Henry Drummond* by J.B. Lyons

*Alan Brown* by A.B. Kingsmill

*Harold N. Segall* by C.G. Roland

*William R. Beaumont* by Julian A. Smith

# CONTENTS

*Acknowledgements* 7

*Introduction* 9

| | | |
|---|---|---|
| One | The Locked Door | 11 |
| Two | Ahead of His Time | 19 |
| Three | Internship, Postgraduate Training, Marriage | 35 |
| Four | World War I and Alan Brown's Battles | 45 |
| Five | Alan Brown's Reign: 1919-1951 | 54 |
| Six | Private Practice | 106 |
| Seven | Private Life | 128 |
| Eight | A Falling Star | 167 |

*Conclusion* 199

*Notes* 201

Appendices:
       1. A selected list of Alan Brown's publications 207
       2. Some sources interviewed and quoted 215
       3. Books and theses consulted 219

*Index* 221

# Acknowledgements

This is essentially an oral history of Dr. Alan Brown. Much of my research consisted of interviews with his family, friends, colleagues, students and patients. I have relied heavily on their strong opinions, some favourable, some critical, but none unprejudiced. The tales they told suggest the alert and wary life they lived when their paths crossed Brown's. Any negative statements about Alan Brown's professional and private life I have rejected unless they appeared independently during the course of other interviews. Those who knew Alan Brown and who were consulted, briefly or at length, have created this portrait of a fine physician but a difficult man.

*His colleagues or students*: Drs. Crawford S. Anglin, George D.M. Boddington, Alan Bruce-Robertson, A. Lawrence Chute, Donald R. Clark, Lillian Sugarman Clark, Mrs. T.G.H. Drake (Nina), Mrs. J. Harry Ebbs (Adele), Drs. Robert Farber, Adelaide L. Fleming (McLeese), Donald Fraser, Miss Grace Haldenby and Mrs. Ruth Haldenby Mulholland, Drs. Robert Haslam, W.A. Hawke, Ross Johnson, Margaret Forbes Kaufman, RN, Drs. Bernard Laski, Eric C. H. Lehmann, Helen N. McCallum, RN, Drs. Keith MacDonald, Howard (Pete) McGarry, Frances Mulligan (McKay), Robert L. MacMillan, Margaret D. Neilson, RN, Phyllis Norton, RN, Drs. M. Justin (Gus) O'Brien, Walter F. Prendergast, C. Philip Rance, Helen Reid (Chute), Donald C. Robertson, Colin S. Ross, Morton

Shulman, Nelles Silverthorne, John J. Slavens, J.A. Peter Turner, Frederick Weinberg.

*His family, friends, or patients*: Nancy Baker Boxer, Barbara Robertson Elliott, H. Stephen Gooderham, Ann Kelley Griffiths, Barbara Alan Brown Kelley, Timothy A.G. Kelley, Elisabeth Fisher Lawson, Barbara Ross McEwen, Eluned Carey-Evans MacMillan, Nancy Alan Brown Mayer, Jennifer O'Brian Somerville, Mrs. Frederick F. Tisdall (Mary), Charles Tisdall, Constance Sparrow Trusler, Bunt Smith Walker, Stephanie Kelley Woods.

*Professional*: Blair Fraser, lawyer. Homewood Health Centre. HSC (Hospital for Sick Children) Public Affairs: Claudia Anderson. HSC Library: Elizabeth Oleryk and staff. HSC Women's Auxiliary Archives: Diane Gilday. Photographs: H.W. Tetlow (courtesy *Maclean's Magazine*) and City of Toronto Archives.

Constructive criticism came from members of my family (especially W.G.K. and Suzanne Kingsmill) who were not allowed to reject my requests for their advice and assistance.

Unless otherwise stated, photographs are courtesy of Alan Brown's family.

# Introduction

*"I've worked for five guys at Sick Kids and each one has had something to contribute, but none — **none** as colourful or as frustrating as Brown!"*
Dr. J.A. Peter Turner

Dr. Alan Brown was not an ordinary man. He was a man of extremes. As Chief of Paediatrics at The Hospital for Sick Children for thirty-two years he infuriated some and instilled reverence in others. At the hospital he demanded immediate obedience to his orders. At home he gave none. With his young patients he was gruff but gentle; with parents, cruel. Mothers left his office in tears. In the hospital he was a dictator and a bully, famous for his scathing sarcasm. Anyone who did not meet the high standards of competence and dedication that he demanded was fired. Whether he had the right to do so or not is irrelevant. He did it.

Throughout most of his life, he was a man ahead of his time; he even arrived in the world four weeks before he was expected. He was the first Canadian doctor to seek extensive postgraduate training in paediatrics by studying in Europe and New York. After four years of intensive study abroad he returned to Toronto in the spring of 1914 as the country's first academically and clinically qualified paediatrician. He was a superb diagnostician and a vehement advocate of preventive medicine in the days when the practice of "crisis medicine" took precedence.

Printed in the United States
39461LVS00006B/235-408